STANDARD AMERICAN 21

The Rubber Bridge Player's Guide for the Twenty-first Century

by
John Sheridan Thomas

SECOND EDITION
January 2006

© Copyright 2004 John S. Thomas
All rights reserved. No part of this publication may be reproduced, stored in a retrieval
system, or transmitted, in any form or by any means, electronic, mechanical, photocopying,
recording, or otherwise, without the written prior permission of the author.

Note for Librarians: A cataloguing record for this book is available from Library and Archives
Canada at www.collectionscanada.ca/amicus/index-e.html
ISBN 1-4120-2063-8

*Printed on paper with minimum 30% recycled fibre. Trafford's print shop
runs on "green energy" from solar, wind and other environmentally-friendly power sources.*

Offices in Canada, USA, Ireland and UK
This book was published *on-demand* in cooperation with Trafford Publishing. On-demand
publishing is a unique process and service of making a book available for retail sale to the
public taking advantage of on-demand manufacturing and Internet marketing. On-demand
publishing includes promotions, retail sales, manufacturing, order fulfilment, accounting and
collecting royalties on behalf of the author.

Book sales for North America and international:
Trafford Publishing, 6E–2333 Government St.,
Victoria, BC v8т 4р4 CANADA
phone 250 383 6864 (toll-free 1 888 232 4444)
fax 250 383 6804; email to orders@trafford.com
Book sales in Europe:
Trafford Publishing (uκ) Limited, 9 Park End Street, 2nd Floor
Oxford, UK oxi 1нн UNITED KINGDOM
phone 44 (0)1865 722 113 (local rate 0845 230 9601)
facsimile 44 (0)1865 722 868; info.uk@trafford.com
Order online at:
trafford.com/03-2642

10 9 8 7 6 5 4

Special thanks to Marian, my wife, who shouldered the brunt of editing of this book; but more important, for her patience during the year it took me to determine how to integrate a variety of contemporary bidding ideas into a rational and cohesive "bidding system", and to write the text.

ABOUT THE AUTHOR

John Sheridan Thomas devoted most of his professional career to management consulting, as an associate with Booz Allen Hamilton, New York, NY then as a partner of Devonshire Associates, Cambridge, MA. He is the author of the widely acclaimed "So Mr. Mayor, You Want to Improve Productivity . . . ", published in 1974 by the National Commission on Productivity in cooperation with the Ford Foundation.

Mr. Thomas has been playing bridge since 1950. After years of casual play, he became a serious student of the game, a bridge teacher (accredited by the American Bridge Teachers Association and the American Contract Bridge League), and a club director.

Many of the bidding methods embodied in **Standard American 21** were tested and validated through application of probability statistics and analysis of millions of random deals (computer-assisted of course - a tool not available when Goren and his contemporaries worked out bidding rules on table napkins). Mr. Thomas was the first bridge authority to:

- Recognize the explicit value of a good five-card suit to notrump contracts.
- Define more precise bidding sequences exploiting the full potential of five-card majors.
- Quantify the large advantage weak two bids have over their predecessors, the strong two openers and strong jump overcalls.

Mr. Thomas authored a variety of bridge articles published in the **ABTA Quarterly** and in **Bridge Today**. He publishes **Bridge Snaps**, an e-mail letter of bridge tips and humor. Here in **Standard American 21** he presents an integrated bidding system built upon Goren's basics of 50 years ago, bringing together the best and most widely recognized innovations since then. This contemporary bidding system is in some ways simpler than the early standard, and in a great many ways more precise.

He is a graduate of the Mercersburg Academy and the University of Pennsylvania.

THE SECOND EDITION

This second edition contains cosmetic and editorial changes to add clarity (some might say "to eradicate fuzziness") here and there and to make the text more attractive. Bridge is a complicated subject so, it seems to me that anything that makes it easier to read and understand is all to the better. I hope these changes accomplish this.

This edition also contains a significant change in bidding preference with respect to notrump openers. Not long after the five-card major concept was introduced some forty years ago, experts disagreed and continue to disagree as to the better choice when a hand qualifies to open a major suit and 1NT. Spurred by Marty Bergen's advice in his book **Points Schmoints** where he wrote "Always open 1 NT - even with a five-card major" and determined to resolve this issue once and for all time, I systematically tested and compared consequences of either choice. The finding, included in this edition, is that Bergen has it right - notrump openers, without exception, produce superior results by a small but significant margin.

CONTENTS

INTRODUCTION

It has been said that some people have natural card sense. Applied to bridge, that means they have an instinct for the right timing and sequencing of card play. This notion has validity with respect to card play, but it clearly has little to do with bidding because this requires the coordinated effort of two partners. To put it another way, great expertise is of little consequence when playing in an inferior contract; finding the best contract is the essential prerequisite to winning bridge; and this requires knowledge and consistent application of a rational bidding system by both members of a partnership. For rubber bridge players, herewith is that rational bidding system for the twenty-first century.

In the winter of 1931, a team assembled by Ely Culbertson defeated another prominent team including Oswald Jacoby. This win propelled the Culbertson system of bidding into prominence in the bridge world. Culbertson's system based on honor tricks declined in the 1930's and nearly disappeared in the 1940's, as it was superseded by Charles Goren's point-count system. Goren was first to present a complete, integrated point-count bidding system in his book **Contract Bridge Complete**. The Goren system rapidly grew in popularity to the point where it became universally known (in North America) as Standard American. In the early postwar years, Standard American prevailed. Top American players using it were among the most prominent names in the game: Becker, Crawford, Lightner, Mitchell, Rapee, Schenken, Silodor, and Stayman. Year after year those players won world championships for the United States.

Standard American was not only the system of experts, it was the system used by every bridge player. It was a delightful era for bridge; you could sit at a bridge table with anyone and not have to ask "do you play . . ?" because virtually everyone played by Goren's rules. As every bridge player knows, employing a common bidding system does not guarantee uniform results. Far from it. The possible combinations of cards dealt, player skills, and other variables are nearly infinite so there is lots of room for diversity of expertise and for highly skilled practitioners to obtain superior results.

Over the second half of the 20th century, experts created a multitude of new treatments and artificial methods (conventions) primarily for the duplicate bridge game. Thus to play tournament bridge successfully, you need to understand these artificial bidding sequences to know what your opponents are up to. Fortunately duplicate players have regular partners, and they can dedicate the time to develop their own particular set of bidding methods, conventions and nuances, however making changing partners a significant event.

Recreational players often vary partners as the moment requires. Partnership flexibility requires a common bidding system with few variations and even fewer conventions. Moreover casual players are not prone to invest the time it takes to learn and practice complex systems, so naturalness and simplicity are essential ingredients. These are two prime objectives of **Standard American 21**.

There have been outstanding advances in the art of bidding, advances that have been time-tested and proven effective. The early standard has not kept pace. Consequently rubber bridge players lack a modern bidding system suitable for this game. Duplicate players' drive to excel has produced some great ideas that are compatible with rubber bridge and that can enhance it's quality. Some of these fit into the mold of natural bidding. A few though are conventional, involving use of artificial bids. Introduction of five-card majors in particular has had a far-reaching impact on nearly every aspect of bidding. **Standard American 21** adopts the best and most widely used of these modern bidding tools. It is the twenty-first century version of Goren's popular system.

Hand Evaluation

It is widely recognized that the early point-count standards undervalue many hands. **Standard American 21** incorporates two new hand evaluation components to increase accuracy. One measures values of trump length, while the other measures the contribution of a good five-card suit to notrump contracts. These supplemental rules are essential to precision bidding. However a caveat is in order here - they may result in contracts that require a considerable degree of proficiency in the play of the hand, contracts that novices often are unable to make.

Five-Card Majors

The five-card major rule, where opening a major suit promises at least five cards, has been nearly universally adopted in North America. Responses to major suit openers make maximum use of the knowledge that partner has at least five. Three-card support for partner's opening major is adequate to raise. A jump raise describes a hand that is precisely strong enough to play a nine-trick contract when partner has a minimum opener. Likewise a jump directly to game also is as it implies - "partner, I have just enough to contract for game opposite a minimum opener". The impact of five-card majors ripples throughout the bidding structure, affecting many bidding sequences beginning with a minor and to some extent notrump as well.

Stayman And Jacoby Transfers

To achieve precision bidding in notrump, two long-standing conventions, Stayman and Jacoby Transfers, are employed. These have achieved wide acceptance throughout most of the bridge world. Stayman in particular is so pervasive that it is included in beginning bridge classes. Both are easy to learn and they facilitate bidding in many common situations, the mark of good conventions.

Opening Bids At The Two-Level

A major departure from early standards is the use of opening suit bids at the two-level. In the early standard, these bids, 2♣ through 2♠, were natural bids describing strong unbalanced hands with very good holdings in the named suit. Now the conventional 2♣ opener replaces these strong bids, freeing up 2♦, 2♥ and 2♠ to describe preemptive-type hands.

The Two Club Convention creates an opportunity to compete with single-suited weak hands. They occur much more frequently than strong hands (twenty times as often), so 2♦, 2♥ and 2♠ openers are much more productively employed. Otherwise in the earlier environment these shapely hands had to be passed. William S. Root, a world-class bridge player and master bridge teacher in his era, wrote in **Common Sense Bidding** "Weak two-bids and the strong artificial two-club openings are far superior to strong two-bids, and perhaps one day they will be standard with all players". Now they are.

Notrump

In earlier times notrump hands were classified into four groups according to their strength. Each group had a 3-point range (16 to 18, 19 to 21, 22 to 24, and 25 to 27). Hands were evaluated counting only high-card points. Thanks in part to the Two Club Convention, notrump hands now are classified into five groups such that beyond the first level, each group has a range of only 2 points, measurably increasing bidding accuracy.

Recognition of distribution points in evaluating notrump hands also increases accuracy, permitting hands to be opened 1NT which heretofore were considered too weak for this treatment.

Other Changes

There are subtle changes in point-count requirements for specific bids. These changes are neither whimsical nor empirical; they are supported by logic and analysis; and they contribute to greater precision in modern bidding.

*   *   *   *   *

Standard American 21 presents a modern, integrated contract bridge bidding system. The entire system can be adopted quite readily by players of intermediate skills and beyond. Herein rubber bridge players have the tools to achieve real precision bidding from part-score through game and slam. Even so, bridge is not a simple game and try as we may to make it so, good bridge play still requires study and practice, as it always has.

1
HAND EVALUATION

Point-count standards decree that game requires 26 points. This is not to say that 26 points will always produce game. What is meant is that you should bid game when your partnership has 26 points and a satisfactory strain in which to play, even though you will not always make it. Good bridge players will make game with 26 points most, but not all of the time. (A good target is 80%.) But just what are points? When the 26-point requirement was established, it was based on evaluation standards popularized by Charles Goren. These early standards had two dimensions: high-card points to measure the trick-taking value of aces, kings, queens and jacks; and distributional points to measure the trick-taking value of short suits for ruffing tricks and long suits for slow tricks after opponents' holdings in that particular suit are exhausted. These traditional standards were the bases for defining game and slam requirements; and they continue today to provide the foundation for hand evaluation.

Traditional Standards

Traditional standards include values for honors and distributional characteristics. One of the considerable attractions of these standards is their simplicity.

Honor Points

Honor points are derived from face cards. By and large honors take most of the tricks so it is natural to assign considerable value to them. Points are assigned to each honor held and the total of these points comprise a hand's honor-point value. The value scale is:

Ace . . . . 4 points
King . . . . 3 points
Queen . . . . 2 points
Jack . . . . 1 point

There are 40 high-card points in the deck, 10 in each suit and average of 10 in each hand. Aces are actually worth a bit more than 4 points each. Thus it is reasonable to add a point when you hold three or four aces. When you hold an intermediate honor such as a king or queen, and your left-hand opponent (LHO) bids that suit, he is likely to hold a higher honor behind you so that the value of your honor is diminished. Deduct a point. Alternatively intermediate honors may increase in value when the right-hand opponent (RHO) bids a suit in which you hold combinations such as K-x, K-J-x. In these instances, the odds are that some of the missing honors are in front of you and your honors are more likely to take tricks. Add a point as appropriate.

Conventional wisdom says you need 37 points to bid a grand slam, 33 points to bid a small slam, and 26 points to bid game in notrump or a major suit. These are good targets as confirmed by these three dream hands, replete with high cards that illustrate the relationships between honor values and the bench-mark targets.

A) ♠ A K Q J   B) ♠ A K Q   C) ♠ A K Q 9 5
    ♥ A K Q   ♥ A K Q   ♥ A K Q
    ♦ A K Q   ♦ A K Q   ♦ A 5 4
    ♣ A K Q   ♣ K Q J 10   ♣ A 4

Hand A is a lay-down grand slam containing 37 high-card points. Hand B is a sure small slam with 33 high-card points. With 26 high-card points, hand C will produce a game in spades with just a little luck in trump distribution. (Please note that the hands shown here have all of the honors in one hand, whereas in actual practice they are the combination of honors held in both partnership hands.)

The point of these dream hands is to illustrate the close correlation of honor points to game and slam requirements. For balanced hands, honor points are quite reliable in predicting the ability to make games and slams.

Distribution Points

Holding lots of trump cards is beneficial because it facilitates drawing trump, and enables ruffing when declarer's side suits are exhausted. Sometimes small cards in long side suits produce additional tricks after opponents' honors are driven out. When playing in a suit contract, a short suit or a void enables you to ruff potential losers in the other hand. Yet another value of a short suit is to limit losers; assuming you have adequate trump, you should not lose a trick in a void suit. An important contribution to making contracts involves avoiding losers while developing winners, a particular contribution of short suits. All of these possibilities comprise an environment where short suits are good and so are long ones. Obviously length and shortness are interconnected: when you have length in one suit, you also have shortness in another. This is particularly important because hand evaluation standards use short suits to value shortness and also as proxies for length elsewhere.   Points accredited to short suits are:

> Void . . . . .3 points
> Singleton . . . . .2 points
> Doubleton   . . . . .1 point

As the opening bidder, and the most likely declarer, you may include distribution points in your hand, and continue to count them as long as your suit appears to be a viable trump strain. As the bidding proceeds, amend your values if for some reason another suit or notrump becomes a more likely end point. To illustrate, suppose you hold:

♠ 9
♥ A K 7 5 4
♦ K J 3 2
♣ 9 8 3

This hand has 11 high-card points. When contemplating opening, you may add 2 points (tentatively) for the short spade suit. Unless partner supports hearts or diamonds, the value of the short spades may disappear.

When responder has adequate support, he also may count distribution points from his side suits. However with inadequate support, he should not count shortness until there is clarification as to the strain. Also singleton honors or short suits containing an honor, such as K-x or Q-x, often are not worth their combined honor and distribution values. In these situations count the honor value or distributional value, but not both.

When your trump suit has a length of six or more and is supported by partner or is self-supporting, traditional standards fall short. Consider this unlikely hand:

♠
♥ A K 10 9 8 7 6 5 4 2
♦ 8 6
♣ 7

It has just has 7 high-card points and 6 distribution points. Yet played in hearts, most often it will take ten tricks with no help from partner.

This hand demonstrates that traditional distribution points do not measure the full potential of long trump holdings. Here the trick-taking strength is equivalent to 26 points but the hand counts to but 13 points.

There have been a variety of hand evaluation schemes proposed to overcome this problem. Some suggest that assigning short suit values in the primary hand is not appropriate because shortness does not take tricks. The assumption here is that long trump cards will take tricks whether or not they are used for ruffing. This of course is a correct but rather limited viewpoint, overlooking two important distributional characteristics: (1) short suits prevent losers, allowing time to develop slow winners; (2) short suit values are proxies for length in other suits.

There is a trend toward assigning points for length rather than shortness. This idea has merit since we know that somehow more points must be awarded for skewed distributions. However, the traditional method of assigning values to shortness are so widely known and employed, there appears to be no compelling reason to abandon it. The recommended way to improve accuracy without aborting tradition is to add two length measures whose values readily can be demonstrated. These are measures for trump length and measures for qualifying five-card suits in notrump.

Trump Length

To improve accuracy in bidding suit contracts, points must be credited for long trump suits. As the example on page 7 suggests, length beyond five cards, or eight in the combined partnership holdings, generates additional trick-taking values. Nearly always, each trump card beyond a 5-3 or a 4-4 fit produces an additional trick and is worth 2 points. Thus add 2 points for each trump card beyond eight. When responder supports a major suit opening, an eight-card fit is assured. If the primary hand has more than five trump, or if the secondary hand has more than three trump, 2 points may be added for each additional trump held by either partner.

South	South opens 1♥. After partner raises to
♠ A 7	2♥, South counts 13 high-card points, 2
♥ K 10 9 5 3 2	for two doubletons, and 2 for the sixth
♦ A Q 6	heart, 17 in total. This is worth a game
♣ 10 6	try so South invites by calling 3♥.

When you have a long and self-sustaining trump suit, that is a suit that requires no help from partner to control and draw trump (no more than one loser), you may add two points for each card beyond five even though partner has not supported your suit. For example, the sixth card in this suit (A-K-Q-10-8-5) is worth two distribution points, and this seven-card suit (K-Q-J-10-5-3-2) is worth four distribution points with minimal support from partner.

This same principle applies to minor suits, but keep in mind that opening a minor does not promise five cards as it does in a major. Assume a minor opener contains four cards, then as responder you may add two points when you have five of that suit, providing of course you intend to contract in that suit.

Qualifying Suits In Notrump

In Goren's initial hand-evaluation rules, notrump hands were valued entirely by high-card points. Distribution points were not allowed mainly because short suits have no inherent value in notrump. Nevertheless distribution make a difference and some twenty years ago Goren modified his position, writing: "Although no points are allowed for distribution, it is conceded that a long suit is a decided asset and that game may be made with a point or two less when a good suit is held." This is a vague admission and simply adding a point for a fifth card when considering a notrump contract is not particularly accurate. An in-depth analysis of expert play has determined more precisely what conditions contribute to winning nine tricks with less than 26 high-card points. When the partnership had 24 high-card points, they made nine tricks slightly more than one-half of the time. However whenever either partner had a five-card suit with at least three honor points, 68% to 77% of the time nine tricks were taken with 24 high-card points; but absent a good five-card suit, nine tricks were taken only 10% to 21% of the time. These findings have been reconfirmed by a study of hundreds of random computer deals.

The inescapable conclusion is that a good five-card suit is an advantage worth 2 points; a poor one is of no added value. A good five-card suit is one that contains at least three high-card points, such as Q-J-x-x-x or K-x-x-x-x or better. These suits are referred to as _qualifying_ suits. Suppose you hold this hand and partner opens 1NT (with 16 to 18 points):

♠ K 9 5   You have 8 high-card points plus 2 for the
♥ 6 4   qualifying diamond suit. With 10 points
♦ K 9 5 3 2   opposite a 1NT opening, you are good
♣ Q 8 4   enough to jump to 3NT.

The traditional response would be 2NT, an invitation to game. However recognizing that the diamond suit qualifies for 2 more points, the combined partnership values are at least 26 points and 3NT should be bid. This hand is South in **Deal Number 1** (see page 10).

DEAL NUMBER 1

Dealer: North
Vulnerable: None

                          NORTH
                          ♠ A J 7
                          ♥ K 8 5 3
                          ♦ A 10
                          ♣ A 10 6 3

WEST   **EAST**
♠ Q 8 2   ♠ 10 6 4 3
♥ Q 10 9 7 2   ♥ A J
♦ J 6   ♦ Q 8 7 4
♣ J 9 2   ♣ K 7 5

                          SOUTH
                          ♠ K 9 5
                          ♥ 6 4
                          ♦ K 9 5 3 2
                          ♣ Q 8 4

West	North	East	South
	1 NT	Pass	3 NT ///

With 16 high-card points, North opens 1NT. South has just 8 high-card
points. However when he adds 2 points for the qualifying diamond suit,
there is enough combined strength for game so he leaps directly to 3NT.

East leads a diamond. North over-takes West's ♦J to prevent a heart lead
from West. North leads the ♦10, allowing East's ♦Q to hold the trick. Now
declarer has four diamond tricks. East's best lead is the ♥A then ♥J to try
to establish West's hearts. But North wins with the ♥K, returns to dummy
via the ♠K, runs three diamonds, then successfully finesses spades to produce the ninth trick and game - four diamonds, three spades, one heart,
and one club.

Qualitative Considerations

Point-counting is not an absolute value system. There are other factors that contribute to the partnership's trick-taking ability, especially those that enhance partnership compatibility. Here are five common situations that may enhance the value of your hand.

1) When both partners hold honors in the same suit, their combined value is enhanced. Normally this is a side suit that one partner has bid.

You	Partner	These holdings are complementary.
♥ K 10 6 5	♥ Q J 9	This suit will deliver three tricks after the ace has been driven out.

2) In either hand, honor cards in the same suit, such as K-Q-x, are more productive than the same honors in two different suits.

A)	♠ A K 6 5 4	B)	♠ A Q J 7 5
	♥ 9 4 3		♥ 7 6 2
	♦ K 10 3		♦ K Q 6
	♣ Q 5		♣ 7 5

Both of these hands contain 12 high-card points. However hand B is stronger because the king and queen are in the same suit.

3) Honor cards in long side suits help develop slow tricks in that suit. When you can draw the entire suit, perhaps conceding a trick along the way, your spot cards can produce additional tricks beyond the hand's point-count value.

♠ A K Q 7 5	With spades trump, quite often the
♥ 9	diamond suit can produce one or two
♦ A K 6 4 3	slow tricks. The two high honors
♣ Q 3	make this possible.

4) Intermediate card sequences, such as J-10-9 or 10-9-8, sometimes can produce additional tricks, although they have no honor values, or nearly none.

You	Dummy	With only 5 honor points, if the
♥ A 7 6 5	♥ J 10 9 2	outstanding honors are divided, you should take three tricks by leading from the dummy to your hand, twice if necessary.

5)   Shortness, especially a void or singleton, can pay off big opposite quick losers in the other hand.

You	Dummy	If dummy has sufficient trump
♥ 6 3 2	♥ (void)	support, these three losers can go away quickly by ruffing.

Quick Tricks

High cards that usually win the first and second round of a suit are referred to as quick tricks. In competitive bidding auctions, you may need to appraise the hand in terms of offense strength verses defense strength. For instance, when you have a good offense (lots of tricks if you get to name trump) but poor defense (lack of quick tricks when the opponents name trump), you may want to compete in the auction more aggressively than when you have very good defensive holdings. Quick tricks also are crucial when contemplating penalty doubles.

```
Ace . . . . . . . .. . . . . . . . . . . . . . . . . . . . . .1 quick trick
Ace and King in the same suit   . . . . . . . . . .2 quick tricks
Ace and Queen in the same suit   . . . . . . . .1 1/2 quick tricks
King and Queen in the same suit . . . . . . . . .1 quick trick
King and one or more spots . . . . . . . . . . . .1/2 quick trick
```

Games And Slams

In a major suit contract, eight trumps and 26 points comprise the primary criteria for bidding game; as does 26 points and a stopper in every suit in notrump. Being a game of probabilities, competent players will make game most, but not all of the time when their hands satisfy these criteria. Naturally some deals will produce game with less when the defenders' cards are favorably located, or when the two declarer hands compliment each other especially well. Game and slam criteria are:

```
Game in notrump (9 tricks) . . . . . . . . . . . . . 26 points
Game in a major suit (10 tricks) . . . . . . . . . 26 points
Game in a minor suit (11 tricks) . . . . . . . . . 29 points
Small slam (12 tricks) . . . . . . . . . . . . . . . . 33 points
Grand slam (13 tricks) . . . . . . . . . . . . . . . . 37 points
```

Notrump requires nine tricks for game while a minor suit requires eleven. Thus the usual practice is to prefer notrump and to proceed to a minor suit only when it is evident that 3NT is not viable. However, major suit contracts are often safer than notrump when either hand is unbalanced.

The bonus for a small slam is 500 points not vulnerable and 750 points vulnerable. These bonuses are the same for contracts in minor suits, major suits and notrump. The difference in trick values (10 points per trick for a major over a minor, and 10 points for the first trick in notrump over a major) pale in significance as compared to the slam bonus. Consequently at rubber bridge the only important objective is to bid and make slam in the most secure contact. Unlike game contracts, at slam the minors should enjoy equal billing.

The standard to bid for a small slam is 33 points. Nevertheless, reality is that, if you are good at playing the cards, you should expect to make small slams 70% of the time with just 32 points. This observation is especially important when you have 19 points opposite an opening hand; you know that the partnership has 32 points and perhaps more. Usually you have no way to discover when partner has a point or two more than the bare minimum. Consequently you should contract for slams when you find a respectable fit, are sure of 32 points, and have adequate controls. Suppose partner opens 1♠ and you hold:

♠ 7 5 3 2	You have 16 high-card points and
♥ K Q 10 9	and 3 distribution points, for a total
♦ A K 5	of 19, and very good spade support.
♣ A 4	

Your values plus partner's minimum add up to slam. If partner has more than a minimum opener, there may be a grand slam. This is the South hand in **Deal Number 2** (see page 14). As you see in the play, slam is not a sure bet but certainly it is worth the effort.

*   *   *   *

Hand Evaluation - Winning Ways

While traditional point-count standards are the foundation for defining game and slam requirements, they often undervalue hands. Finding the best contracts requires adding values for:
- Suit contracts: two points for each trump beyond nine in the two hands.
- Notrump: two points for a qualifying five-card suit (3+ honor points).

DEAL NUMBER 2

Dealer: West
Vulnerable: North/South

NORTH
♠ A K 10 9 4
♥ J 3
♦ Q J 8 7
♣ Q 8

WEST
♠ Q 8
♥ 7 4
♦ 10 9 6 2
♣ J 10 9 7 2

EAST
♠ J 6
♥ A 9 6 5 2
♦ 4 3
♣ K 6 5 3

SOUTH
♠ 7 5 3 2
♥ K Q 10 8
♦ A K 5
♣ A 4

West	North	East	South
Pass	1 ♠	Pass	2 ♥
Pass	2 NT	Pass	3 ♦
Pass	4 ♦	Pass	4 NT (1)
Pass	5 ♦ (2)	Pass	6 ♠ ///

(1) Blackwood. (2) One ace

North opens a spade. South counts 16 high-card and 3 distribution points
giving the partnership a combined total at least 32 points. South does not
need to describe his strength, already knowing the contract will likely be
six or seven spades. He bids 2♥ (forcing) to learn more about North's hand.
North's 2NT call indicates a minimum hand and five spades. South forces with
3♦ then goes on to 4 NT asking for aces. Missing one ace, South settles for
The small slam.

East leads the ♣3 to dummy's ace. Declarer must discard the club loser in
dummy on his fourth diamond, but not before drawing trump. If he loses a
trump, likely he will also lose a club and a heart. He leads trump to his ace,
both defenders following. To finesse or not? He returns to dummy with a
diamond and leads another trump. When West plays the ♠Q, North must
over-take. East's ♠J falls under his king and the contract is safe, providing
he gets rid of the club loser before giving up a heart to the ace.

2
PRIMARY TOOLS

As encompassed here, primary tools include opening suit bids at the one-level, first responses, opener second bids, and second responses. These common bids are employed in subsequent chapters in the contexts of major and minor suit bidding. This redundancy is purposeful - to give the reader a good understanding of these tools and then how they apply in specific bidding circumstances.

There are of course two objectives in the bidding: first to find the partnership's best strain (that is best suit or notrump if a good suit is not forthcoming); and second to determine how high to bid (how many tricks you are willing to try for). With respect to finding the best suit, look for an eight-card trump suit or better. Usually this consists of a 4-4 fit or a 5-3 fit, both combinations produce nearly identical success rates.

OPENING BIDS

In principle, you may open any one of the four suits at any level from one to seven. Each level carries a different meaning with respect to strength and distribution. Opening bids above the one-level are specialized bids described elsewhere (in chapters 8, 9, and 10). Here we focus on suit openers at the one-level. Auctions that start with a bid of 1♣ through 1♠ occur on the order of 80% of the time, hence they are crucial to success at the bridge table.

An opening bid of 1♥ or 1♠ promises a five-card suit. As tempting as it may be, you should not open a four-card major; you will have an opportunity to mention that major later in the bidding. The five-card major rule is one of most significant advancements of the past half-century. (This slow pace of change is mostly good news because it allows you to develop a sound grasp of the subject without fear that your hard-earned knowledge soon will be obsolete.)

15

Open when your hand satisfies opening strength requirements, and that includes hands of 4-4-3-2 distribution where the two four-card suits are majors. There are times when you must open a three-card minor because you have neither a five-card major nor the strength and balance required of notrump. Nevertheless, in most instances you will find that your opening suit is four or five cards in length.

Minimum Openers

The game target is 26 points. Consequently someone must begin with 13 points otherwise both partners might pass out and a game missed. Include distribution points in your opening count, but be prepared to adjust those values.

♠ Q 6 5 3	You have a flat hand with 13 high-card
♥ K 5 2	points. This is a minimum opener. Bid
♦ A Q 9 7	1♦.
♣ Q 6	

In close calls, the most reliable guide for deciding whether or not to open is the modern "Rule of 20". This rule says: when your total high-card points added to the total length of the two longest suits equals 20 or more, open the bidding.

♠ 9 6 5 2	To open or not, that is the question. You
♥ A K J 8 6	have 11 high-card points and 9 cards in the
♦ Q J 10	two longest suits, for a total of 20. Open 1♥.
♣ 5	This hand is South in *Deal Number 3* (see page 17) where a good game was found.

Holding a minimum opener with two biddable suits, the general rule is to open the higher-ranking suit then bid the lower-ranking suit next.

♠ Q 8 7 6 4	This minimum opener has length in
♥ K Q 8 4 3	both majors. Open spades, and then
♦ A 5	call hearts next. This allows partner
♣ 4	to return to your spades at the same level.

An underlying consideration is that, in the trump suit, length is more important than honors because trump spots nearly always produce tricks, and _honors produce tricks whether or not they are trump_.

The most difficult case is when your two suits are spades and clubs. If you open spades and partner responds 2♦ or 2♥, you must go to the three level to mention the five-card club suit, a bid which shows a

DEAL NUMBER 3

Dealer: South
Vulnerable: None

NORTH
♠ A 4
♥ Q 9 7 2
♦ A 6 5 4
♣ 8 6 4

WEST
♠ J 10 8 3
♥ 10 5
♦ 8 3 2
♣ A Q J 7

EAST
♠ K Q 7
♥ 4 3
♦ K 9 7
♣ K 10 9 3 2

SOUTH
♠ 9 6 5 2
♥ A K J 8 6
♦ Q J 10
♣ 5

West	North	East	South
			1 ♥
Pass	4 ♥ / / /		

South, the dealer, has 11 high-card points. Should he open the bidding? Applying the "rule of 20" (11 high-card points plus 9 cards in hearts and spades = 20), he decides the hand qualifies to open. North evaluates his hand and finds 13 dummy points in support of hearts. He jumps directly to game.

It does not matter what West does. South has just three losers - a club, the diamond finesse, and a spade. Two spades are ruffed in the dummy.

very strong hand. Holding five clubs and five spades, the practical solution is to open spades only when they are good enough to bid again. Partner will expect a six-card suit, so your five-card suit should be better than average - such as A-K-9-7-5, A-Q-J-9-7, or K-Q-J-10-3. Otherwise, pretend you have only four spades and open 1♣.

Maximum Openers

When considering opening a strong hand, you want to be sure not to miss game. Partner is expected to pass with less than 6 points. Consequently if you open at the one-level with 21 points or more, game might easily be missed when partner passes with 4 or 5 points. Thus the nominal upper limit for a suit opener at the one-level is 20 points. You may open with more than 20 points if your hand cannot take 8 ½ tricks or if you need to conserve bidding space. Otherwise, strong hands should be open 2♣ (see Chapter 8: Two Club Convention).

> ♠ A K Q 6 5   You have 19 high-card points plus 1
> ♥ 9 6   for distribution. Open 1♠.
> ♦ A Q J
> ♣ K 8 2

The offensive strength of this hand is eight tricks: five spades (if they behave), two diamonds, and another diamond or a club. You need to find partner with three spades and 6 honor points (an ace and queen for instance) to be able to take ten tricks. It is safe to open 1♠ because game is unlikely unless partner responds.

Some hands stronger than 20 points are close calls where a one-level opening is better than a strong two club. Two-suited hands may be better opened at the one-level to allow room to explore both suits. Also there are hands that have more than 20 points yet need at least 6 points from partner for game; thus there is no need to open with a forcing bid.

> A)   ♠ A Q J 5 4   B)   ♠ K Q J
>   ♥ A 6   ♥ A K J 6 2
>   ♦ 6   ♦ A 6 5 4
>   ♣ A K J 8 6   ♣ K

Both of these hands are strong and unbalanced, but they should be opened at the one-level. With hand A you may need to explore two suits as possible trump, and need bidding space to do this. Open 1♠ followed by 3♣ (a reverse bid showing extra strength) Hand B has 21 high-card points but it has five losers. Open 1♣. If partner cannot respond, it is unlikely that you can make 4♥.

Fourth Seat Openers

Opening in the fourth seat involves some considerations beyond the 13-point criteria. Holding a strong hand of 16 points or so, there should be no hesitation about opening - chances are your side has well over half of the honor points, so there is no risk to opening and you should always do so. However when you have a minimum opener, the decision is not so obvious. Since no one else has opened, the outstanding honors must be divided nearly evenly around the table, and your side is not likely to have a game combination. In assessing whether or not to open a minimum hand in fourth seat, the following conditions should be taken into account.

First, to open a minor surely invites the opponents into the auction, and likely their suit is superior to yours. When the opponents control spades, they win the contract nearly every time (or else you bid too high), and you wish you had passed out and gone to the next deal.

West	North	East	South	South Hand
Pass	Pass	Pass	?	♠ 10 5
				♥ K 9 7
				♦ Q J 9 5 4
				♣ A Q J

South has 13 high-card points, enough to open. However, with the honors dispersed around the table and lots of spades and hearts unaccounted for, the odds are 2 to 1 in favor of the opponents finding a major fit and winning the contract at any level to which they wish to compete. If you open a diamond in fourth seat with this minimum hand, any good coming from that action will be in favor of your opponents.

Second, when you have a major suit, the hand most appropriately belongs to your side, especially when you have defensive values in spades. Open these hands with 13 points or more any time a partial game score is worth playing for.

A)	♠ A Q J 5 4	B)	♠ A Q 6
	♥ 6 2		♥ K J 7 6 4
	♦ 8 7		♦ 7 6 3
	♣ K Q 6 5		♣ Q 7

Both are minimal openers and you can expect the outstanding honors to be dispersed among the three other players. Hand A controls spades. Hand B has the heart suit and good defensive values in spades.

FIRST RESPONSES

Generally the responder is obliged to control the bidding process, deciding when to continue and when to stop. The way you control this process is through the rules regarding forcing and non-forcing bids. The general concept is that open-ended bids (where the hand value implied by a bid is too broad for partner to reasonably place the contract) are forcing, and limit bids (where the hand value implied by the bid is limited, usually within 2 or 3 points) are not forcing. First and most important, a new suit by responder is forcing. Please note, however, that a notrump response is not a new suit, thus not forcing.

When contemplating how to respond to a one-level opener, it is useful to classify your hand into one of these three categories:

Minimum Strength . . . . 6 to 9 points
Invitational Strength . . . . 11 to 12 points
Game Strength . . . . 13 + points

The logic of these ranges should be apparent. They are derived from the game target of 26 points. Partner opens with at least 13 points. Adding 13 points in your hand and the partnership has met the game requirement. With a little less, 11 to 12 points, you are close to game (invitational) and partner needs very little extra to satisfy the game target. The minimum range of 6 to 9 points is broader, but you have plenty of bidding space below game to distinguish the better from the poorer.

A minimum hand is worth only one free bid. The second bid, if any, should follow partner's direction, such as to show a preference between two suits, or perhaps to accept an invitation to game. As responder, your first thought should be: "can I support partner's suit?" Holding a modest hand show your support promptly.

An invitational hand allows you to approach game, but not to bid it unless partner shows a little extra potency. Two common ways to show invitational hands are: jump raise from one to three when you have support; bid 2NT at your first or second opportunity.

Holding game strength, you have a number of bidding choices to distinguish different distributional configurations. With adequate support or balance, jump directly to game in a major suit or notrump. Needing more information about partner's hand, bid a new suit, biding time to find the best contract.

New Suits

When you bid a new suit, it is forcing so you may do so with 6 points or 25 points or anywhere in between, certain of another bid.

1)

Partner	You	♠ A K 10 4 3
1 ♥	1 ♠	♥ A 2
		♦ K J
		♣ 6 4 3 2

You have a good 15 high-card points opposite an opening bid. Even though this is enough for game, you do not yet know where to play it. The 1♠ response buys time to discover more about partner's hand.

2)

Partner	You	♠ 3 2
1 ♣	1 ♥	♥ A 7 6 5
		♦ K 9 6 5
		♣ 10 3 2

The most common response is to call a new higher-ranking suit at the one-level. You may do this with a four-card suit. Here the preferred practice is to skip over diamonds and call hearts, else you may find that, when the bidding returns to you for a second call, it has advanced beyond your ability to compete, and you may have missed a 4-4 heart fit.

First responses at the two-level _require_ 10 points. This rule is intentionally restrictive. You may have a good diamond suit but only 8 points when partner opens 1♠. Since you may not mention diamonds at the two-level with 8 points, respond 1NT.

A)	♠ 5 4	B)	♠ 5 4
	♥ K 5 2		♥ A J 7
	♦ K Q 8 7 6		♦ K 9 8 7 6
	♣ 9 6 5		♣ Q 6 5

Both of these hands have the same distribution, but hand A has only 8 high-card points while hand B has 10 high-card points. Partner opens 1♠. You have only two spades so a raise is not appropriate. Holding hand A, you are too weak to bid 2♦ and have no recourse but to call 1NT. Although hand B has a less attractive diamond suit, 10 points is sufficient to call 2♦.

Raises

When you have support for partner's opening suit, you may raise or jump raise. Major suits require three-card support, assuring the partnership of a 5-3 fit. Minors require four-card support, but the preferred practice is to defer a minor suit raise with less than five-card support except in competitive bidding. Five-card support usually produces a nine-card fit in a minor. _Direct raises are limit bids, and are not forcing_. Point count standards for direct raises are:

- The single raise (from 1 to 2) promises 6 to 9 points.
- The jump raise (from 1 to 3) promises 11 to 12 points.
- The double jump raise (from 1 to 4) promises 13 to 14 points.

Yes, there is a gap between the single raise (6 to 9 points) and the jump raise (11 to 12 points). A 10-point hand is not good enough to jump to the three level, because it too often falls short of nine tricks, unless it is a very good 10 points. You can make life easier for partner by down-grading so-so 10-point hands and upgrading those that contain some special features that make the hand more attractive.

1)   *Partner*   *You*   ♠ J 10 5
        1 ♥   2 ♥   ♥ Q 8 7
                                     ♦ K 8 4
                                     ♣ A 9 6 5

This is a typical 10-pointer. However, these unsupported honors in a flat hand are rather suspect. Raise to 2♥.

2)   *Partner*   *You*   ♠ 9
        1 ♦   3 ♦   ♥ K 8 6
                                     ♦ K Q 8 3 2
                                     ♣ 9 8 7 3

This is a good example of a jump raise in a minor suit. The hand is worth 12 points in diamonds. There is no other attractive choice but to jump raise, showing an 11 or 12 point hand with very good diamond support.

3)   *Partner*   *You*   ♠ K 7 6
        1 ♥   4 ♥   ♥ Q J 6
                                     ♦ 10 2
                                     ♣ A K 9 7 6

You have good heart support and game values opposite partner's heart opener. The direct jump to 4♥ precisely discloses 13 to 14 points and heart support, and does so without giving away information to the opposition.

Jump Shifts

Jump shifts occur when you respond in a new suit at one level higher than necessary. For instance, partner opens 1♦ and you have a strong hand and a good spade suit you want to show. If you call 2♠, this is a level higher than necessary as you could have said 1♠. The purpose of this jump shift is to describe a very strong hand, and to force the bidding to game. The strength defined by a responder jump shift is 17 to 18 points. When you have 17 or 18 points opposite an opening hand, the partnership is within 2 points of slam strength (17 in your hand and 13 in opener's hand). If the opener has more than a minimum, he should recognize the potential and strive to find a good slam contract. After the jump shift, continue to describe the distributional character of your hand, but in a passive way so as to allow partner to select the final contract.

1)	*Partner*	*You*	♠ A Q 3
	1 ♦	3 ♣	♥ 8 2
			♦ K 7 6 5
			♣ A K 8 6

This hand has 16 high-card points, a distribution point, and quality diamond support; a good candidate for the jump shift. You expect to play the contact in diamonds, or perhaps notrump. This hand is South in ***Deal Number 4*** (see page 24). It is an excellent illustration of how, after a jump shift, the opening partner is able to steer the bidding into a good slam.

2)	*Partner*	*You*	♠ A J 3 2
	1 ♥	3 ♣	♥ 9 7
			♦ K J
			♣ A K J 6 4

Jump to 3♣. This 17 high-card point hand can accommodate any second bid by partner. If she next bids 3♦, follow up with 3 NT; or raise any other bid to game.

It is not imperative to jump shift just because you have 17 or 18 points. Sometimes you need to conserve bidding space to learn more about partner's holdings. A good time to consider this approach is when you have two suits of five cards or more. You may want to bid both of them without accelerating the pace. Usually it works out best to bid the higher-ranking suit first because then you are more likely to be able to bid the second suit, forcing of course.

DEAL NUMBER 4

Dealer: North
Vulnerable: All

NORTH
♠ K 10 7
♥ A K J 7
♦ A Q J 9 2
♣ 9

WEST
♠ J 9 6 5 4
♥ Q 9 6 4
♦ 3
♣ Q 10 2

EAST
♠ 8 2
♥ 10 5 3
♦ 10 8 4
♣ J 7 5 4 3

SOUTH
♠ A Q 3
♥ 8 2
♦ K 7 6 5
♣ A K 8 6

West	North	East	South
	1 ♦	Pass	3 ♣
Pass	3 ♥	Pass	4 ♦
Pass	4 NT (1)	Pass	5 ♥ (2)
Pass	5 NT (3)	Pass	6 ♥ (4)
Pass	7 ♦ ///		

(1) Blackwood for aces. (2) Two aces. (3) Blackwood for kings.
(4) Two kings

North opens a diamond. South values his hand, counting 16 high-card points and 1 distribution point. He jump shifts, advising partner of his strength. With his excellent hand, North realizes that a slam is in the works, perhaps a grand slam. North calls 3♥, a reverse to show 4 hearts and 5 diamonds. South raises diamonds, confirming that diamonds are to be trump. North takes charge, employing Blackwood to discover that the partnership has four aces and four kings, then signs off at 7♦.

In the play of the hand, North has twelve quick tricks. The thirteenth trick Comes from ruffing a heart in dummy.

Partner	You	♠ A Q 10 8 7
1 ♦	1 ♠	♥ A 7
1 NT	2 ♣	♦ J
2 ♦	3 ♣	♣ K Q J 6 3

With partner holding opening strength, you can safely push to game - in notrump if nothing else attractive turns up. The advantage of this sequence is it quantifies your five spades without bidding them twice. The second diamond call carries a strong inference of a five-card spade suit, and surely five clubs.

When you have 19+ points and partner opens, the combined strength is at least 32 points. Assuming adequate controls and a suitable strain, 32-point combinations produce slam 70% of the time, assuming good declarer play of course. Rather than try to describe these big hands to partner, take charge of the bidding. Begin with a new suit and maintain control until an appropriate game or slam contract is determined.

Although partner expects 17 to 18 points from you when you jump shift, you may make this bid with stronger hands, as a means of describing distribution and great strength. This may deceive partner who, when holding a minimum, will likely pass out any game bid you make. Consequently you are the one who must continue to force the bidding to slam, unless of course you decide not to go for it.

Notrump Responses

Following an opening suit bid, your first charge is to determine if there is an eight-card fit. Even though your hand may be suitable for a notrump response, first show a four-card or better major if you have one. Notrump responses are selected when you have neither a good fit in partner's suit nor a higher ranking four-card major. Hence notrump responses deny holding a four-card major (exception: a 4-3-3-3 flat hand). Invariably these are nearly balanced hands. Notrump responses describe both strength and balance. Respond 1NT with a minimum (6 to 10 points), and jump to 2NT or 3NT with larger hands.

Partner	You	♠ A 6
1 ♦	1 NT	♥ 8 7 4
		♦ 10 4 3
		♣ Q 8 7 4 2

This hand has a meager 6 points, too weak for 2♣; hence 1NT is the right response.

The jump to 2NT is game invitational, requiring 11 to 12 points, but as with the 1NT response, it is usually preferable to show a four-card major first.

Partner	You	
1 ♦	2 NT	♠ A 5 3
		♥ 9 7 6
		♦ 10 5 4
		♣ A K 8 5

This balanced 11 point hand is accurately described by a jump to 2NT. The partnership has at least 24 points, producing eight tricks most of the time. If partner has at little extra, 3NT should be a very good try.

As you should expect, the jump to 3NT reflects opening strength of 13 to 15 points, a fairly balanced hand with a stopper in each unbid suit.

Partner	You	
1 ♥	3 NT	♠ A K 2
		♥ Q 3
		♦ K 8 6 5
		♣ Q 8 7 6

This hand contains 14 high-card points, the right amount to contract for game opposite an opening bid. In making this bid, you have also conveyed to partner that in addition to being balanced, you have less than four spades and only two hearts.

Passed Hands

If you had previously passed, a new suit call is no longer forcing. Having passed, you have already limited your hand to a maximum of 12 points. If by chance partner's opener enables you to upgrade your hand to 13 points or so, jump directly to game in notrump or in his suit if you can. It is highly unlikely that you could reach for game in some other suit in these circumstances so the new suit forcing rule is void here. Also it should be apparent that if you do respond in a new suit after initially passing, it had better be a good one because partner has no obligation to continue.

1)	Partner	You	
		Pass	♠ A K 7 4 3
			♥ A 2
	1 ♥	1 ♠	♦ 8 5 3
			♣ 6 4 2

With these good values, bid spades. Partner has a variety of second-bid options, but he may pass, leaving you to play spades.

2)   *Partner*   *You*   ♠ A 10 3
                         Pass   ♥ 9 2
        1 ♥   2 NT   ♦ A 8 5 3
                                       ♣ K 9 4 2

With 11 high-card points, your hand is a little light to open. You cannot
support partner's hearts but the hand is suitably balanced for notrump.

OPENER REBIDS

The opening bid is the first step toward describing your hand. The
suit selected tells something about distribution, and opening at the one
level broadly defines your strength as 13 to about 20 points. Most often
partner responds with a new suit, in which case his hand may be 6 points
or strong enough for slam. This is an open-ended response, thus forcing
for one round. When you make the second call, it should be such that it
narrows the strength range and further defines distribution. The rebid you
select should narrow your strength to within two or three points.

Minimum Rebids

Partner calls a new suit in response to your opening bid. The
nominal range for a minimum hand is 13 to 15 points. The nominal range
for intermediate hands is 17 to 18 points, leaving it entirely up to your
discretion as to what to do with the 16-point orphans.

1)   ♠ A Q J   *You*   *Partner*
        ♥ 10 8 7   1 ♦   1 ♥
        ♦ K Q 8 7   1 NT
        ♣ Q 5 2

Partner's hearts may be only four long, so notrump looks like the best
strain. At any rate, there is no game unless partner bids again..

2)   ♠ Q J 10 5 3   *You*   *Partner*
        ♥ K J 10   1 ♠   2 ♦
        ♦ 10 7   2 NT
        ♣ A Q 10

When partner responds at the two-level, you may skip over your suit and
bid 2NT when your suit is not good enough to warrant a rebid.

3) ♠ J 7   *You*   *Partner*
    ♥ K Q J 7 5 4   1 ♥   1 ♠
    ♦ A 8 4   2 ♥
    ♣ Q J

This 2♥ bid shows no more than a minimum opener and suggests that
you have a six hearts.

4) ♠ Q 10 8 6   *You*   *Partner*
    ♥ A J 8 5 4   1 ♥   1 ♠
    ♦ K Q   2 ♠
    ♣ K 2

When partner's response is a major and you have four, raise to show the
4-4 fit. This raise promises four-card support.

5) ♠ J 2   *You*   *Partner*
    ♥ A Q J 5 3   1 ♥   1 ♠
    ♦ K Q 7 6   2 ♦
    ♣ 4 2

Partner is able to return you to hearts without raising the bidding level, so
this new suit does not promise more than a minimum. He may of course
have good club stoppers to warrant a try at notrump.

The situation is rather different when responder first bids 1NT
instead of a suit because this immediately limits his hand to 6 to 10 points.
Unless you have more than a minimum, the partnership does not have
enough for game and you should quickly conclude the bidding in whatever
appears to be the best strain.

    ♠ K Q   *You*   *Partner*
    ♥ K 10 9 6 5   1 ♥   1 NT
    ♦ 5 4 3   Pass
    ♣ A J 2

There is no game here. Notrump appears to be as good and perhaps a
better strain than 2♥, and there is no place else to go.

The Reverse Bid

You have a hand valued at 17 or 18 points (the invitational range
for an opening hand) and partner's first response promises 6 points.
Game is feasible if partner has 8 points or more. Often the reverse is the
way to identify this strength and (usually) a 5-4 distribution. Suppose you
open the bidding with 1♣ and partner responds 1♠. If your next bid is 2♦
or 2♥, partner would have to go to the three-level to return to your first-bid

suit. Hearts and diamonds are ranked higher than your initial club opener, this defining the reverse bid. These reverses normally show strength of 17 points, but perhaps a good 16 in a pinch. Reverses are forcing for one round.

♠ A 5	You	Partner
♥ 9 3	1 ♣	1 ♠
♦ A J 10 7	2 ♦	
♣ A Q J 9 4		

This 2♦ is a reverse bid as diamonds rank higher than clubs. Partner would have to go to the three-level to return to your first suit. Normally the first suit contains at least five cards and the second suit four cards.

Jump Rebids

Suppose you open the bidding with 1♥ and partner responds 1♠. You may jump rebid your own suit providing it is a good six-card suit, or jump raise partner's suit. In either case, you should have 17 or 18 points.

1)	♠ A Q J 7 6 5	You	Partner
	♥ 10 9	1 ♠	1 NT
	♦ K Q 7	3 ♠	
	♣ A J		

Partner may have a minimum and that is not enough for game. However if he has about nine points and some support or a balanced hand, he may accept your invitation.

2)	♠ A J 10	You	Partner
	♥ K 9 8 5	1 ♦	1 ♥
	♦ A Q J 6 2	3 ♥	
	♣ 6		

This is a good jump raise. You have very good heart support, an excellent diamond suit, and a singleton club. All values are working.

At times a jump directly to game is appropriate. Your suit must be self-sustaining. Additionally, since partner may have only 6 points you need a good 19 or 20 points.

1)	♠ A K Q 9 6 5	You	Partner
	♥ 10	1 ♠	1 NT
	♦ K Q 9	4 ♠	
	♣ A 4 2		

With this attractive hand containing eight or nine tricks, you should elect to play in game, expecting partner's hand to deliver a trick or two - the diamond ace or two club honors would do quite nicely.

2)   ♠ A 10 9 6   *You*   *Partner*
      ♥ 10 7   1 ♣   1 ♠
      ♦ A Q 2   4 ♠
      ♣ A K Q 3

Here you have 19 high-card points and a 4-4 spade fit. The game raise is direct and descriptive. If partner has values for slam, he is not constrained from proceeding further.

The Jump Shift

When a jump shift is made by the opener, it describes a hand of 19 or 20 points, perhaps 21 in a pinch, and is game-forcing. *This jump shift requirement for an opening bidder is higher than for a responder*.

1)   ♠ A Q 7 6   *You*   *Partner*
      ♥ 9 5   1 ♦   1 ♥
      ♦ K Q J 10 8   2 ♠
      ♣ A Q

You could have bid 1♠ so 2♠ is a jump shift promising 19 points. Typically your distribution in these two suits is 5-4. Partner has at least six points, for a combined total of 25 or more. You should continue to game.

2)   ♠ A Q 4 2   *You*   *Partner*
      ♥ K   1 ♦   1 NT
      ♦ A Q J 10 3   3 ♠
      ♣ Q J 5

This jump shift is quite descriptive, showing 19 or 20 points and probably five diamonds and four spades. Armed with this information, partner should be able to calculate the chances of slam. This hand is North in **Deal Number 5** (see page 31). South has diamond support and pushes on to a diamond slam via Blackwood. This contract is a 50/50 proposition requiring a successful diamond finesse.

3)   ♠ A Q   *You*   *Partner*
      ♥ K Q J 10 4 3   1 ♥   2 ♣
      ♦ A K 6   3 ♦
      ♣ 8 4

DEAL NUMBER 5

Dealer: North
Vulnerable: North/South

NORTH
♠ A Q 4 2
♥ K
♦ A Q J 10 3
♣ Q J 5

WEST
♠ J 10 9 7
♥ 10 9 7
♦ K 5
♣ 8 7 4 2

EAST
♠ 5 3
♥ Q J 6 5 4 3
♦ 9 7 4
♣ A 9

SOUTH
♠ K 8 6
♥ A 8 2
♦ 8 6 2
♣ K 10 6 3

West	North	East	South
	1 ♦	Pass	1 NT
Pass	3 ♠	Pass	4 ♣
Pass	4 ♦	Pass	4 NT (1)
Pass	5 ♥ (2)	Pass	6 ♦ ///

(1) Blackwood asking for aces. (2) Two aces.

North has the values for a jump shift. He opens 1♦, jumps to 3♠ at the second round, then rebids diamonds. Encouraged by the secondary fit in spades and good diamond fit, South goes for the slam after finding that the partnership has three aces.

East leads the ♣A then ♣9, declarer taking with the king in the dummy. Next declarer finesses diamonds twice and draws the remaining trump. By discarding the fourth spade on a dummy's ♥A, declarer has no more losers; making the small slam. Odds of making this slam are 50/50 and declarer is fortunate to find the ♦K on-side.

Slam is a distinct possibility here as you have 19 high-card points and partner's 2♣ bid promises 10. Lacking a four-card second suit, jump in a respectable three-card suit to describe this great strength - you have a strong heart suit to fall back upon so there is little risk in calling diamonds.

SECOND RESPONSES

Partner has opened and then bid a second time after you responded with an open-ended call, that is one that did not limit you strength. You have retained leadership of the bidding process.

Minimum Strength

Minimum strength (6 to 9 points) is just enough for one free response. Usually your first response is a new suit, at the one-level. As far as partner knows, you could have 6 points or 20 points. Since you actually have a minimum, you must make this crystal clear at your second bid. Unless opener has made an aggressive second bid, there is no game in sight, hence your objective is to retire the bidding promptly.

1) | *Partner* | *You* | ♠ 10 9 5 4 |
    |-----------|-------|------------|
    | 1 ♥ | 1 ♠ | ♥ 10 7 |
    | 1 NT | Pass | ♦ K Q J 8 |
    | | | ♣ 8 7 |

This is a minimum hand without heart support. Mention your four-card spade suit to keep the bidding alive. Then as partner's second-round 1NT indicates a minimum, pass.

2) | *Partner* | *You* | ♠ A 8 6 5 |
    |-----------|-------|-----------|
    | 1 ♥ | 1 ♠ | ♥ 9 8 |
    | 2 ♦ | Pass | ♦ Q 9 8 6 |
    | | | ♣ 9 7 6 |

Partner's bidding suggests five hearts and four diamonds, yet only a minimum opener. You have a 4-4 fit in diamonds, and a 5-2 fit in hearts. Pass and let partner declare, that is unless you need 60 points for game, in which case you should return partner to 2♥.

3) | *Partner* | *You* | ♠ Q 4 3 2 |
    |-----------|-------|-----------|
    | 1 ♥ | 1 ♠ | ♥ J 3 |
    | 3 ♥ | Pass | ♦ 8 6 5 |
    | | | ♣ K 7 6 3 |

Partner has a good six-card suit, and is strong enough to jump the bidding - a game invitation which you must ruefully decline having only six high-card points and minimal heart support.

Invitational Strength

An invitational hand is worth 11 or 12 points. When you show this strength, partner will continue to game with marginally more than 13 points. Your second bid identifies this invitational hand.

1)
Partner	You
1 ♥	1 ♠
1 NT	2 NT

♠ K 10 5 3
♥ 8 7
♦ K 7 4
♣ A Q 8 7

This balanced 12 point hand is within a fraction of game. The raise to 2NT is descriptive.

2)
Partner	You
1 ♥	2 ♦
2 ♥	2 NT

♠ Q J 7
♥ 8
♦ K 9 7 6 5
♣ K Q 8 3

Perhaps some would be comfortable with passing, allowing partner play a 2♥ contract. Although your 2♦ bid promises 10 points, your hand is actually somewhat better than that. Almost any 14 or 15 points in partner's hand will produce an excellent play for 3NT.

3)
Partner	You
1 ♥	1 ♠
2 ♥	3 ♥

♠ K J 5 4
♥ Q 6
♦ A J 8 4
♣ 5 3 2

Partner rebids hearts to indicate that he has a good six-card suit. Your two hearts to the queen are now sufficient to raise to 3♥. This heart raise has two messages. Beside showing support, it is an invitation to game (why push the contract up one notch otherwise?).

Any time partner's second bid indicates that he has more than a minimum opener, your 11 or 12 points are sufficient for game provided you know where to play the contract. If you do, you may jump directly to that game. If not, try another suit and trust partner to clarify the situation.

1)   *Partner*   *You*   ♠ K 9 7 6
         1 ♣   1 ♠   ♥ J 10 2
         2 ♥   3 NT   ♦ A 6 5
                                   ♣ Q J 8

Partner reverses, promising 17 points. You easily have game power. Having bid diamonds then hearts, partner likely has five diamonds and four hearts.

2)   *Partner*   *You*   ♠ A K 4 2
         1 ♣   1 ♠   ♥ 9 7
         3 ♣   3 ♦   ♦ A 9 8 5
                                   ♣ 7 5 4

Even though there is a 6-3 club fit, with 11 high-card points you should be thinking of notrump. On the other hand, the lack of a heart stopper is troubling. Bid your second suit, diamonds. Now three suits are covered; perhaps partner will find a heart stopper and press on to 3NT.

Game-Going Strength

Sitting in the third or forth seat with opening strength, it is a pleasure to hear partner open. "We have game, maybe slam; where should we play it" is the appropriate thought. Unless you have immediate support for partner's major, you need bidding space to sort out possible contracts. First respond with a new suit, buying time to find out more about partner's hand.

Good trump suits are discovered within two rounds of bidding: partner rebids a six-card suit and you have two for a 6-2 fit; or perhaps partner raises, indicating a 5-4 or 4-4 fit; or perhaps you have four-card support for partner's second suit. However the fit is found, press on to game.

1)   *Partner*   *You*   ♠ A K 9 2
         1 ♥   1 ♠   ♥ J 9
         2 ♥   4 ♥   ♦ A Q 6 5
                                   ♣ 10 5 4

You have game strength and a 6-2 fit in hearts. This is adequate to jump to 4♥, even though partner has a minimum. There is no need to advise the opponents about your diamonds along the way - thus inviting them to lead clubs. (Note: 3♣ is a reasonable choice after partner rebids his hearts, but the only point to this action would be to keep open the possibility of a 3NT contract.)

2)   *Partner*   *You*   ♠ A K 7 6
        1 ♦   1 ♠   ♥ K Q
        2 ♠   4 ♠   ♦ Q 10 6
                                     ♣ 8 7 4 3

Partner supports spades at the second round of bidding. With 14 high-card points and a 4-4 fit in spades, there is no reason to stop below game.

When there is no fit, you still have the option of choosing to play in notrump. Any time partner opens and you have 13 or more points, you should aim for game. If you cannot find a fit, take a chance on 3NT. Stop short of game only when there is an obvious misfit.

1)   *Partner*   *You*   ♠ A 4 3
        1 ♦   1 ♥   ♥ A 8 4 2
        1 NT   3 NT   ♦ 5 2
                                     ♣ K Q J 2

Partner's 1NT places his hand in the minimum 13 to 15 point range. You have enough strength to jump to 3NT and there is no slam in these cards.

2)   *Partner*   *You*   ♠ A K 10 2
        1 ♦   1 ♠   ♥ A 6
        2 ♣   3 NT   ♦ A 8 5
                                     ♣ 9 8 4 3

Three suits have been bid, with partner showing 5-4 in the minors. While you have only one heart stopper, there is an excellent chance that you can run five diamond tricks. If not, partner has a second heart stopper. Although you have a club fit, the odds of making 3 NT are much better than 5♣.

Misfits

As we all know too well, there are times that you cannot find a fit and both hands are too unbalanced to play in notrump. One partner needs to recognize the misfit and stop bidding promptly.

        Partner   *You*   ♠ A Q 9 7 6 5
        1 ♥   1 ♠   ♥ 9
        2 ♥   Pass   ♦ Q 7 6
                                     ♣ 10 9 2

Partner has six hearts (maybe seven). Should you rebid your six-card
spade suit? You just might find partner with two or three spades, making
spades a better trump suit than hearts. But if you rebid spades, partner
will expect a better hand than you have, and without spade support he is
likely to go on to 3♥ or possibly 3NT. Collectively your partnership has
about 20 high-card points, much too weak for a game. Discretion
suggests you pass and let the stronger hand play the 2♥ contract.

When you have a misfit and both parties have long suits and no
support for the other's suit, there is a tendency to bid your suit once too
often, pushing the contract one or even two levels beyond what you can
make. *Avoid competing with partner for the contract*. With minimum
range hands, do not bid a six-card suit more than twice. If there is a
misfit, defer to partner's suit rather than push the contract to a higher
level.

*   *   *   *

Primary Tools - Winning Ways

Bid whenever your hand meets the minimum requirements, otherwise you
will often miss game contracts:
- Open the bidding with 13+ points.
- Respond to partner's opening with 6 or more points.

Responding to a opening bid:
- With a strong hand keep the bidding alive with a forcing bid:
  - ✓ New suit (6 or more points).
  - ✓ Jump shift (17 or 18 points).
- With 19+ points, look toward slam.
- With a weak hand raise immediately if you can.

Stop bidding as soon as you recognize a misfit.

3
NOTRUMP

The approach to notrump bidding continues to parallel Goren's structure, but with considerable refinements since. For one, hand evaluation is more accurate thanks to recognition of the value of a qualifying five-card suit. Another refinement is credited to the Two Club Convention as it reduces most notrump ranges from three to two points. Together these two changes improve notrump bidding accuracy immensely.

Modern **Standard American 21** embraces Stayman and Jacoby Transfer conventions, which are important to the tasks of finding good major suit fits and in placing the declarer in the most advantageous hand. Stayman is presented in Chapter 4 and Jacoby Transfers in Chapter 5.

Balance

Notrump openers should have balanced or nearly balanced distributions. These distributions are 4-3-3-3, 4-4-3-2, and 5-3-3-2 (in any suit order). There should be no singletons and only one five-card suit.

Five-Card Majors

When you have a balanced (5-3-3-2) five-card major and the hand qualifies to open either the major or 1NT, either choice is acceptable. However for those who are proficient playing notrump contracts, the notrump opener is recommended as it more often yields better results. For an in depth analysis of opening notrump compared to a five-card major, see **Note 1: Five-Card Majors vs. Notrump**, page 201.

Stoppers

Stoppers are card combinations that prevent the opposition from winning an entire suit before giving up the lead. The prime combinations are A, K-x, Q-x-x, and J-x-x-x. It is oft-times necessary to relax these rules, thus increasing risk, when it appears that notrump is likely to be the most befitting contract. In a pinch you may consider suits of Q-x, J-x-x or even x-x-x-x as protected. There is some risk of opponents running a suit even when you have a stopper, but you must take calculated risks to win at bridge. It is quite acceptable to open 1NT without a stopper in one suit. When one hand has 16 to 18 points and the other 10 points or so, the total being sufficient to contract for 3NT, it is a rare deal where the partnership has no stopper in the suit an opponent chooses to lead.

The Notrump Advantage

There are two great advantages to opening notrump, especially 1NT. The most obvious one is that notrump more precisely describes hands than do suits. Not so obvious is the preemptive value of notrump; when you open 1NT, you remove all of the one-level bidding space and you intimidate the opposition by declaring strength. Consider this hand:

♠ Q 3	Of course you would open 1♥ with this
♥ K J 7 6 5	hand, but what do you do after RHO
♦ K Q J 9	gets there first opening 1NT?
♣ 8 4	

You have a minimum opener so the idea of overcalling 2♥ behind a known strong hand is daunting; the conservative posture is to pass. The bad news is that, in the actual deal, partner had 10 high-card points and a heart fit good enough the make 4♥. But having passed after RHO opened 1NT, the opponents played and made a 1NT contract.

16 TO 18 POINT HANDS

The most frequent notrump opening is 1NT. This action describes a balanced hand of 16 to 18 points.

1)	♠ K Q 8	This balanced hand has 16 high-card points.
	♥ A Q 10 3	The poor club suit should not deter you from
	♦ K Q 7 5	opening 1NT.
	♣ 7 3	

2) ♠ K Q 2   This is a hand worth 14 high-card points plus
    ♥ 7 5 4   a diamond suit worth 2 more. It is a good 1NT
    ♦ K Q 9 8 7   opener; certainly preferred over diamonds. If
    ♣ A 5   this good five-card suit were a major rather
                     than diamonds, 1NT still would be preferred.

Responses

Conventions are inherent components of notrump responses. In response to a 1NT opening bid, both 2♣ and 2♦ are conventional; thus you cannot use either of these calls to show a natural minor suit. When your hand values 7 points or less opposite a 1NT opener, the prospect of game is quite poor and a pass to play 1NT is usually the best choice. Alternatively when you have a five-card major, the Jacoby Transfer may be used to play a 2♥ or 2♠ contract in the strong hand. In this chapter only natural responses are presented.

Natural Responses With Balanced Hands

Excluding our notrump conventions, the common response is to pass or raise notrump, and the question, then is how high to raise.

1) *Partner*   *You*   ♠ 7 6 5
    1 NT   Pass   ♥ A J 4
                               ♦ Q 9 7
                               ♣ 8 7 3 2

Some hands are not meant to be bid. When partner opens 1NT and you have less than 8 points, the combined strength is less than 26 points.

2) *Partner*   *You*   ♠ Q 8 6 4
    1 NT   2 NT   ♥ A J 9
                               ♦ Q 10 2
                               ♣ 5 4 3

A hand of 8 or 9 points opposite a 1NT opener constitutes invitational strength. When you do the math, you find the partnership assest may add up to 26 points, but not necessarily. The 2NT response is invitational, allowing partner to pass with a minimum, or opt for game with a maximum.

3) *Partner*   *You*   ♠ A 8 7
    1 NT   3 NT   ♥ A J 9
                               ♦ Q 5 4
                               ♣ 9 8 6 5 4

Opposite the 1NT opener, 10 points are sufficient for game. When you are reasonably balanced and have no interest in a major suit, jump directly to 3NT. The upper limit to this jump bid is about 14 points because with 15 or more slam is a distinct possibility (15 points plus 17 or 18 from partner = a good slam try).

Natural Responses When Holding A Major

When you have a five-card major and less than 8 points, game is unlikely and the choice is whether to play in 1NT or two of the major. The major suit is marginally better than notrump, however you must use the Jacoby Transfer to arrive at a 2♥ or 2♠ contract.

With a five-card major and invitational strength (8 to 9 points), there is no natural method to both evaluate game prospects and test for a fit, hence the Jacoby Transfer is employed, this time to show both a five-card major and invitational strength.

With game strength (10+ points), you have a choice of methods and may choose the one that best suits your hand, either transfer or a natural jump bid in the major suit. In choosing which of these two methods to use, the prime consideration is whether it is advantageous to have the lead come into your hand or into partner's hand. If the deal is played in the major rather than notrump, the jump bid will place the contract in your hand whereas the transfer will place the contract in partner's hand. This ability to place the contract in either hand is an important feature of modern bidding.

1)   Partner   You   ♠ K 10 5 4 3
      1 NT   3 ♠   ♥ K 8
                            ♦ K 9 5
                            ♣ 9 4 3

This hand is worth bidding game in either notrump or spades. Because your three kings are vulnerable to leads from your right, it is a good tactic for you to be the declarer, putting LHO in the lead and protecting at least one of your kings from a right-hand lead. Jump to 3♠ This is a game force so partner must raise to 4♠ with three-card support, or bid or 3NT otherwise.

2)   Partner   You   ♠ A 10 9 5 3 2
      1 NT   4 ♠   ♥ 4
                            ♦ K J 6 5
                            ♣ J 7

This hand should be played in four spades since partner's 1NT assures you that he has two spades, for a 6-2 fit. The diamonds will have some protection because you are declarer. The point here is that, whenever you have good reason to prefer the opening lead from LHO into your hand, bid the major suit yourself rather than employ the transfer convention.

Natural Responses When Holding A Minor

The approach with minor suits necessarily differs from majors because so often you are looking for the possibility of a notrump contract before resigning to a minor. Even with a good five-card minor, more often notrump will produce better results. The time to acknowledge a good minor is when there is a possibility of slam, that is when your hand is worth 14+ points opposite a 1NT opener.

1) *Partner*   *You*   ♠ 9 5
    1 NT   3 NT   ♥ 8 6 5
                                 ♦ J 9 5
                                 ♣ A K J 5 4

You have good clubs and little else. The hand is good enough to try for game, but not slam. With a little luck these clubs will produce five tricks in notrump, giving 3NT the edge over 5♣.

2) *Partner*   *You*   ♠ K Q 9
    1 NT   3 ♦   ♥ K 3
                                 ♦ K Q 9 5 2
                                 ♣ Q 10 9

Partner opens 1NT. You have 15 high-card points and a good diamond suit. Even though your comrade may have only 16 points, you are good enough for a slam try. Jump to a game-forcing 3♦. This is the South hand in *Deal Number 6* (see page 42). When North supports diamonds, South continues to 6♦, checking for controls along the way.

Opener Rebids

When responder jumps directly to 3NT, there is nothing more to do but pass and accept the game contract. There are however some few occasions when responder leaves the final decision to you, the opener. A 2NT response, being invitational, is one of these occasions where you are called upon to make the big decision; you should have a maximum 18 points or a quite good 17 points to commit to game.

DEAL NUMBER 6

Dealer: North
Vulnerable: All

NORTH
♠ A 8 2
♥ A Q 7 2
♦ A 10 6 4
♣ A 4

WEST
♠ 10 7 6 5
♥ J 9 8 6 5 4
♦
♣ K 7 3

EAST
♠ J 4 3
♥ 10
♦ J 8 7 3
♣ J 8 6 5 2

SOUTH
♠ K Q 9
♥ K 3
♦ K Q 9 5 2
♣ Q 10 9

West	North	East	South
	1 NT	Pass	3 ♦
Pass	4 ♦	Pass	4 NT (1)
Pass	5 ♣ (2)	Pass	6 ♦ ///

(1) Blackwood. (2) 0 or 4 aces

South has 15 high-card points and a good diamond suit, sufficient for slam. His 3♦ bid is game-forcing, and North has diamond support, encouraging enough to initiate Blackwood. With North showing 4 aces, South goes for the slam.

On a heart lead, South counts 12 tricks if the trumps behave. To protect against a 4-0 trump split, he leads the ♦K. If either opponent shows out, he is able to finesse either opponent for the ♦J. This safety play is successful and 12 tricks are taken, making the slam.

1) ♠ A 10 3   *You*   *Partner*
    ♥ A J   1 NT   2 NT
    ♦ K Q J 7   3 NT
    ♣ Q 8 6 5

This 17-point hand has solid values - two aces, a strong diamond sequence, and good intermediates. Accept the invitation.

2) ♠ J 7 6 5   *You*   *Partner*
    ♥ K Q 8   1 NT   2 NT
    ♦ K J 8   Pass
    ♣ A Q 4

Here you have a minimum 16 points and a flat hand. Pass up the invitation.

Suppose partner responds to your 1NT by jumping to three of a suit. Of course this is game-forcing. He has a five-card suit (or longer) and is wondering if you have support. Holding three-card support in a major, you are expected to proceed to game in that suit. Lacking support, return to 3NT.

    ♠ Q J   *You*   *Partner*
    ♥ A J 2   1 NT   3 ♥
    ♦ K J 8 3   4 ♥
    ♣ K Q 9 2

Partner has five hearts and leaves the final choice to you. Having good heart support, continue on to 4♥.

19 TO 20 POINT HANDS

Opening 1NT requires 16 to 18 points and 2NT requires 21 to 22 points. There is a two-point gap between these two, that is balanced hands of 19 and 20 points. There are two common ways to identify hands valued at 19 or 20 points; the most frequent is the jump shift, which typically is undertaken with a distribution of 5-4-x-x. With a flatter hand, you may show 19 to 20 points by opening a minor then jumping to 2NT.

    ♠ A 4   With 18 high-card points and good clubs,
    ♥ J 8 2   this hand is too strong for 1NT. Open
    ♦ K Q 4   1♣ then jump to 2NT at the next round.
    ♣ A K J 9 4

This hand is the North in **Deal Number 7** (see page 45). Being too strong to open 1NT, North opens 1♣ and jumps to 2NT following South's heart response. South raises to 3NT. The game contract is not a sure thing, but it is worth the try.

There are some situations where you cannot show a balanced 19 or 20 points in the manner displayed above, so you must improvise in one way or anther.

1)
♠ A K 3	*You*	*Partner*
♥ Q J 10 9	1 ♣	1 NT
♦ A K	3 NT	
♣ Q 9 6 2		

Your jump to 3NT is a good move. Since partner promises only 6 points to answer 1NT, you should have some 20 points to contract for game. In this instance you are one point short, but any other bid would mis-represent your hand to a considerable degree.

2)
♠ K J 5	*You*	*Partner*
♥ A 3 2	1 ♦	2 ♣
♦ K Q J 6	3 NT	
♣ A Q 2		

Your most difficult case is to hear partner answer in a suit at the two-level as in this example. He has 10+ points and you have 20 points. Is there a slam? You need only 16 points for this 3NT call, so you are substantially under-bid. The alternative is to make a forcing reverse (still an under-bid) or jump shift to 3♥, which accurately defines your strength but misleads partner about your distribution.

21 TO 22 POINT HANDS

Balanced hands of 21 and 22 points are described by opening 2NT. These hands are nearly strong enough to take 8 tricks without help from partner.

1)
♠ Q J 9 8	You have a balanced hand of 21 high-
♥ A J	card points. Open 2NT, describing this
♦ K Q J	to a tee. If there is a 4-4 spade fit,
♣ A Q J 3	partner can find it using Stayman.

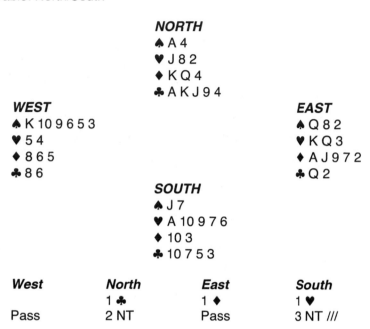

DEAL NUMBER 7

Dealer: North
Vulnerable: North/South

	NORTH	
	♠ A 4	
	♥ J 8 2	
	♦ K Q 4	
	♣ A K J 9 4	

WEST		**EAST**
♠ K 10 9 6 5 3		♠ Q 8 2
♥ 5 4		♥ K Q 3
♦ 8 6 5		♦ A J 9 7 2
♣ 8 6		♣ Q 2

	SOUTH	
	♠ J 7	
	♥ A 10 9 7 6	
	♦ 10 3	
	♣ 10 7 5 3	

West	North	East	South
	1 ♣	1 ♦	1 ♥
Pass	2 NT	Pass	3 NT ///

North values his hand at 18 high-card points and 2 more for the good club suit. Standard bidding is to open a suit then jump to 2NT. East overcalls 1♦ but, with two diamond stoppers, this does not deter North from no-trump. South stretches a bit for the game.

North is declarer and receives a diamond lead from East. North's plan is to establish hearts for four tricks, plus two clubs, two diamonds and one spade. He takes the first diamond in hand, then leads the ♥J. East covers with the queen, dummy's ace winning. Now declarer drives out the ♥K, and East leads another diamond to establish the rest of the suit, but it is too late. Declarer runs hearts and takes the top clubs and ♠A, making nine tricks. East could make life more difficult for declarer by switching to spades when he wins the heart trick. Unable to get a second diamond trick, declarer tries for a third club trick. If he finesses clubs, he loses: if he plays the ace and king, the queen falls and ♣J becomes his ninth trick.

2)   ♠ K J 9   This hand is sufficiently balanced for
        ♥ A J   notrump and has stoppers in all suits.
        ♦ A Q 9 7 6   Open 1NT.
        ♣ K Q 3

Responses

When partner opens 2NT, it is up to you to lead the partnership into the best contract. Just a few points are enough to try for game and you have available the notrump conventions, Stayman and Jacoby Transfers, to help. Any natural response you make is forcing to game. The only way to stop below game, other than pass, is to use the transfer, forcing partner to call a major, after which you may pass to play at the three-level. With a balanced hand and 4 to 9 points, raise directly to 3NT.

Partner	You	♠ 7 5 4
2 NT	3 NT	♥ A 9 4
		♦ 10 8 6 5 4
		♣ 6 5

You have 4 high-card points and partner has 21 or 22. The total is within a single point of game. Do not be shy; game is worth the try.

With a six-card major, prefer to play in the major. You may jump directly to game if you want to become declarer.

Partner	You	♠ Q 9 8 5 4 3
2 NT	4 ♠	♥ 6 5
		♦ K 8 2
		♣ 4 2

You are sure of an eight-card fit and most of these spades will produce tricks in a spade contract. By jumping directly to 4♠ you protect your diamond king from attack by RHO.

Any time you have 11 points or more, the partnership has at least 32 points and you should aim for slam. Notrump slam bidding is presented in detail in Chapter 12.

23 TO 28 POINT HANDS

The Two Club Convention is used for balanced hands of 23 points or more. Since this convention also is used for strong unbalanced hands, it is the opener's second bid that identifies the hand as being of the notrump type. The Two Club Convention is presented in Chapter 8 so here we merely present how this convention fits into the notrump structure. Here are three bidding sequences by which the opener describes strong, balanced hands.

1)   ♠ A K Q 9   *You*   *Partner*
     ♥ A 6   2 ♣   2 ♦
     ♦ K Q 6   2 NT
     ♣ K Q 8 5

Opening the strong two club announces strength. When followed by 2NT, it announces a balanced hand of 23 or 24 points.

2)   ♠ A K 8   *You*   *Partner*
     ♥ A Q 9   2 ♣   2 ♦
     ♦ K Q J   3 NT
     ♣ K Q J 5

This rare hand of 25 or 26 points is described by a jump rebid to 3NT after the two club opener.

3)   ♠ A K Q J   *You*   *Partner*
     ♥ A 2   2 ♣   2 ♦
     ♦ A K Q 6   4 NT
     ♣ K Q 10

This sequence identifies a balanced hand of 27 or 28 points if you are ever fortunate enough to hold one.

SLAM INVITATIONS

The slam invitation in notrump occurs any time 4NT is called immediately following a natural notrump bid at a lower level. It's purpose is to suggest that you, the 4NT caller, have sufficient values for slam when partner has better than a minimum within whatever range he has promised. It's utility is limited because all notrump ranges beyond the !NT opener are two-point ranges, and it is a marginal exercise to ask partner to bid slam with 22 points (for instance) or pass 4NT with 21 points. Thus this slam invitation is recommended only after a 1NT opener where there is a three-point range, and even then the Gerber convention asking for aces and kings may be more useful an approach to notrump slams. (See notrump slam invitations in Chapter 12.)

Partner	*You*	♠ J 5 4
1 NT	4 NT	♥ A 9 4
		♦ K Q 10 9
		♣ A J 6

You have 15 high-card points and want to play in 6NT, but only if partner has more than 16 points. Following this slam invitation, partner may pass with a minimum and should raise to 6NT with 17 or 18 points.

*   *   *   *

Notrump - Winning Ways

When considering notrump, include the value of a qualifying five-card suit, and open notrump whenever the hand qualifies even when you have a five-card major:

- Open 1NT with a balanced 16 to 18 points.
- Open a suit then jump with a balanced 19 or 20 points.
- Open 2NT with a balanced 21 or 22 points.
- Open 2♣ with a balanced 23+ points.

When responding to notrump:

- If you are not interested in a suit contract, add up the combined assets and:
  - ✓ With near-game strength, invite to game (2NT).
  - ✓ With game strength, bid the game (3NT).
  - ✓ With near-slam strength, invite to slam (4NT).
- If you are interested in a suit contract and want to become declarer:
  - ✓ With a six-card major, bid the game.
  - ✓ With a five-card major, bid 3 of your major.

4
THE *STAYMAN* CONVENTION

In the early bridge era some very good hands caused anguish because they were so difficult to bid satisfactorily. (Some still do, but not as many!) One such type was the balanced hand of 16 to 18 high-card points containing a four-card major of some potential. Experience made it apparent that these hands often produce equal or better results playing in the major when there is a 4-4 fit rather than in notrump. When you play in notrump, there is the risk that the defenders may establish and run their best suit while you are unable to ruff as you might in a suit contract. Thus ruffing losers sometimes gives an edge to suit contracts.

When you open 1NT with a balanced distribution, eighty percent of such hands contain a four-card major. The Stayman Convention was devised to enable responder, holding a four-card major, to determine whether opener also has four of the same suit. If he finds this so he guides the partnership into a major suit contract instead of notrump.

The Stayman Convention was invented by George Rapee. His frequent bridge partner, Sam Stayman wrote an article about it in *The Bridge World*, June 1945, and his name stuck with the convention ever since. This convention is quite useful and widely accepted, earning a permanent place in *Standard American 21*.

Imagine this conversation between two bridge partners if they could simply talk their way through the bidding:

> West: "I have a strong, balanced hand."
> East: "Do you have a four-card major? If you do, which suit is it?"
> West: "I have four spades."

East now knows whether or not there is a 4-4 fit in spades, and he is able to place the contract accurately - in the major if there is a fit, in notrump if

49

not. Of course our bidding vocabulary is restricted to just 15 legal words, so we need to translate this conversation into bridge lingo. West opens the bidding 1NT ("I have a strong balanced hand"). East, having enough values to respond and a four-card major, bids 2♣, a conventional bid initiating Stayman (thus saying to partner: "Do you have a four-card major? If you do, which suit is it?"). West answers by bidding his four-card major ("I have four hearts/spades"), or by bidding 2♦ ("I do not have a four-card major"). At this point East knows partner's strength (16 to 18) and whether or not there is a 4-4 fit in one of the majors.

Sitting opposite a 1NT opening, you should have a minimum of 8 points for the partnership to reach a total of 26 points. With 8 or 9 points, there is a possibility, but not a certainty, of game strength. This is an invitational hand. With 10 points or more, you have game strength. Stayman may be employed in either case providing you have a four-card major.

Responder Has Invitational Strength

Partner opens 1NT. Add the value of your invitational hand (8 or 9 points) to partner's 16 to 18 points and you find that the partnership assets are at least 24 points, and perhaps as many as 27 points. You could bid 2NT, leaving it to partner to decide on part score or game. But if you have a four-card major, you may want to check for a 4-4 fit. After asking for a four-card major, you should like to announce "partner we have (or do not have) a 4-4 major, but I do not have quite enough strength to go on to game".

1)

Partner	You	Partner	You
♠ A 6 5	♠ 9 4	1 NT	2 ♣
♥ 9 5 4	♥ K 8 7 6	2 ♦	2 NT
♦ K Q 6 2	♦ A J 8 5	Pass	
♣ A K 4	♣ 7 5 3		

Partner opens 1NT. Having an invitational hand of 8 points and four hearts, you respond 2♣ (Stayman). Partner's 2♦ bid denies a four-card major, so you complete the invitational process with 2NT. In this case partner has a minimum 16 points and declines the invitation to game.

2)

Partner	You	Partner	You
♠ K 6 5	♠ 9 2	1 NT	2 ♣
♥ Q 8 7 4	♥ K 6 5 3	2 ♥	3 ♥
♦ K Q 3 2	♦ A J 6 4	4 ♥	
♣ A K	♣ 10 4 3		

When you find the partnership has a 4-4 heart fit, your 3♥ bid confirms this fit and invites to game. With more than a minimum 16 points, partner accepts the invitation.

3)

Partner	You	Partner	You
♠ A K 3 2	♠ 9 4	1 NT	2 ♣
♥ J 5 4	♥ K 8 7 6 2	2 ♦	2 ♥
♦ K 6	♦ Q J 8	4 ♥	
♣ A K 4 2	♣ Q 5 3		

You have an invitational hand and five hearts. You can describe this hand with Stayman. First respond 2♣. Partner indicates he has no four-card major. Now you can show both features, invitational strength and five hearts by bidding 2♥. Liking your hearts and having more than a minimum opener, partner accepts the heart game.

Responder Has Game Strength

You have at least 10 points, enough to insist on a game contract. And again you have a four-card major.

Partner	You	Partner	You
♠ A K 6 5	♠ 7 3	1 NT	2 ♣
♥ Q J 6	♥ K 8 5 4	2 ♠	3 NT
♦ K 8 2	♦ A J 7 3		
♣ A 9 8	♣ Q 6 4		

You invoke Stayman looking for a fit in hearts, and partner bids 2♠. Unfortunately this is the wrong suit, so you proceed directly to 3NT

Occasionally you find partner holding four cards in both majors. With luck he mentions the suit you hold so you have no need to know about the other four-card major. Luck is not always the good kind, so sometimes he mentions the one you do not have.

Partner	You	Partner	You
♠ A 7 6 4	♠ 8 5	1 NT	2 ♣
♥ Q J 7 3	♥ K 10 8 6	2 ♠	3 NT
♦ K Q 7	♦ A J 6 5	4 ♥	
♣ A 4	♣ Q 8 5		

Partner announces his four-card spade suit, and you naturally bid 3NT intending to play there. However partner figures that you have hearts since you declined to support his spades. Thus he confidently calls 4♥.

Perhaps you hold a four-card major along with good five-card minor. With game strength you have some bidding room to explore both suits.

Partner	You	
1 NT	2 ♣	♠ K 9 7 6
2 ♦	3 ♣	♥ 10 8 7
		♦ 8
		♣ A Q J 9 4

First try Stayman for a spade fit, intending to go on to 4♠ if you find it. If you do not find it, show the good club suit. *Any time you mention a new suit following Stayman, it must be a five-card suit, never four.*

With 5-4 In The Majors

Suppose you have five hearts, four spades and invitational strength, and partner opens 1NT. Standard bidding has no way to handle this situation. Stayman enables you to find either a 5-3 or a 4-4 fit, while keeping the bidding below game.

Partner	You	
1 NT	2 ♣	♠ Q 9 8 5
2 ♦	2 ♥	♥ K 10 6 4 3
		♦ J 8 6
		♣ 4

Partner's 2♦ signals that he does not have a four-card major. Next your 2♥ bid is a clear statement that you have an invitational hand with five hearts. (Partner knows you would not mention a four-card major after he denied either major.) At this point partner decides whether to play in hearts (if he has three of them) or in notrump; and he decides whether to play in part-score (2♥ or 2NT) or game (4♥ or 3NT).

When you have a similar hand but game strength, use the same sequence, however jumping to the three-level. This of course is a game-force where partner must chose between 3NT and 4♥.

Responding To Two Notrump Openers

A 2NT opener defines a balanced hand of 21 to 22 points. Here Stayman works nearly the same as it does following a 1NT opener. The difference is that there are no invitational sequences. Any response to 2NT is game-forcing - so you should have 4 or 5 points to respond. A Stayman 3♣ response takes you to game, either 3NT or four of a major.

Partner	You	♠ Q 10 5
2 NT	3 ♣	♥ K 7 4 3
3 ♥	4 ♥	♦ 6 4 3 2
		♣ 8 7

You have a minimum hand and a poor doubleton, making it worth looking for a heart fit. Partner shows four hearts and you have found the 4-4 fit.

Responding To A Balanced Two Club Opener

The Two Club Convention accommodates balanced hands of 23 points or more. A balanced hand of 23 or 24 points is identified by opening 2♣ then bidding 2NT at the next round. This sequence is:

Partner	You	♠ K 10 8 5
2 ♣	2 ♦	♥ 9 6
2 NT	3 ♣	♦ K 6 5
3 ♥	3 NT	♣ 9 7 6 5

Partner opens a strong 2♣ followed by 2NT, telling you he has 23 or 24 points and a balanced hand. Your two kings are enough to commit to game, but you might prefer to play in 4♠ if partner has four of them. Invoke Stayman with a 3♣ call, thus finding partner with four hearts. Not being the suit you were hoping for, settle for 3NT.

Responding To Stayman After An Opponent Interferes

Sometimes an opponent interferes with your Stayman process. If you are still able to show a four-card major, do so. Otherwise pass.

You	LHO	Partner	RHO
1 NT	Pass	2 ♣	2 ♥
??			

You were about to reply to partner's request for majors when RHO overcalled 2♥. You have two choices. Bid 2♠ if you have four spades or pass if you do not.

When Is It Stayman?

Stayman is initiated by bidding clubs following a 1NT or 2NT bid by the strong partner. This applies to notrump opening bids and notrump overcalls. Additionally Stayman applies following a 2♣ - - 2NT sequence by the opener (see Chapter 8: The Two Club Convention).

There are three exceptions to these rules. One is when partner opens 1NT and your right-hand opponent overcalls or doubles. In these situations Stayman is "off" and you can bid clubs naturally if you wish.

Another exception is when either partner bids a suit (natural) before notrump is called. The most common sequence here is where the strong hand opens 2♣ (conventional) and responder makes a positive suit response (any call except the conventional 2♦ negative response) When this occurs, continuation of natural bidding enables the partnership to find major suit fits if there are any, and Stayman is "off".

The third exception is that jump bids in clubs by responder (in response to 1NT for instance) are not Stayman bids. They are either natural calls or they initiate the Gerber Convention.

When Not To Invoke Stayman

You should not be surprised to discover that Stayman should not be selected automatically every time you have a four-card major and 8 plus points. You always have the choice to use Stayman or to ignore your major in favor of notrump. Here you have a hand of 9 high-card points and four hearts, and partner opens 1NT. Some automatically employ Stayman without thought to shape, thus bidding to a game in hearts with a hand like this.

Opener	Responder	
1 NT	2 ♣	♠ Q 7 2
2 ♥	3 ♥	♥ K 5 4 3
4 ♥		♦ 9 8 7
		♣ K J 4

An informed player would not bid as this responder does. The hand is North in **Deal Number 8** (see page 55). In the play, declarer manages to win 3 spades, 4 hearts and 2 clubs, but eventually losing 3 diamonds and the club ace for down one. However if North bypasses Stayman in favor of 2NT, the deal will be played in 3NT where declarer easily takes nine tricks on a likely spade or club lead, unless the defense luckily finds a diamond shift very early. Notrump contracts create game swings (3NT making, 4♥ or 4♠ down one) far more often that do major suits when responder has a flat hand (4-3-3-3). _When responder has a flat hand, he should prefer notrump over a 4-4 major, and therefore not engage Stayman._

*   *   *   *

DEAL NUMBER 8

Dealer: East
Vulnerable: North/South

NORTH
♠ Q 7 2
♥ K 5 4 3
♦ 9 8 7
♣ K J 4

WEST
♠ J 10 6 4
♥ 7 6
♦ K J 3
♣ 10 8 7 5

EAST
♠ 9 5
♥ J 10 8
♦ A 10 6 5
♣ A 6 3 2

SOUTH
♠ A K 8 3
♥ A Q 9 2
♦ Q 4 2
♣ Q 9

West	North	East	South
		Pass	1 NT
Pass	2 ♣ (1)	Pass	2 ♥ (2)
Pass	3 ♥	Pass	4 ♥ ///

1) Stayman. 2) Four hearts.

South has 17 high-card points and four cards in both majors, an excellent 1NT opener. North has invitational strength (9 points) and four hearts. He invokes Stayman to try for a 4-4 heart fit. Finding the heart fit, North then invites to game in hearts. North accepts.

West leads the ♠4. South wins with the ♠A and draws trump in three rounds. Next he plays clubs to drive out the ace. East wins the club trick and switches to diamonds (nothing else looks attractive at this point). Declarer is down one, losing three diamonds and the ♣A.

With his flat hand (4-3-3-3), North would be advised to avoid Stayman in favor of notrump. Against a 3NT contract, West leads a fourth spade or a club, giving declarer a very good chance of nine tricks. When East wins the ♣A, he is more likely to return partner's lead than switch to a low diamond, in which case declarer makes nine tricks and game.

The Stayman Convention - Winning Ways

Use Stayman to find a 4--4 major suit, by bidding:
- ✓ 2♣ after a 1NT opener or overcall.
- ✓ 3♣ after a 2NT opener or after a 2♣ - - 2NT sequence.

When your partner initiates Stayman:
- Bid a four-card major if you have one.
- Otherwise bid 2♦ or 3♦.

Do not use Stayman when you have a flat hand (4-3-3-3).

5
JACOBY TRANSFERS

American bridge players first became exposed to transfer bids by way of an article in *The Bridge World* in 1956 by Oswald Jacoby, several years after Goren wrote the script for Standard American. Elegant in it's simplicity and functionality, the transfer bid is a worthy addition to any form of bridge play. Transfers enjoy such broad acceptance that most bridge players are conversant with them, so perhaps those who are not should be.

Partner opens 1NT. You have a five-card heart suit that may make a better contract than notrump if partner has three or four hearts. Absent the transfer convention, you would respond hearts at whatever level appropriate to your strength, becoming declarer whenever the notrump opener supports your hearts. At times, though, it is more profitable for the strong, opening hand to become declarer because this keeps his honors hidden from the defense; and it results in the opening lead coming into the stronger hand. The transfer does this and it is a simple procedure. Any time you respond to 1NT with a 2♦ or 2♥ bid, opening partner is compelled to bid the next higher-ranking suit.

Partner	You	
		♠ K 3
1 NT	2 ♦	♥ Q 10 8 7 5
2 ♥		♦ A 7 2
		♣ Q 9 2

Here you want partner to be first to call hearts, so you respond 2♦. Partner must bid 2♥, the next higher-ranking suit. This is not the end of the auction; but if you do settle for a heart contract, the strong hand becomes declarer.

What if your suit is spades instead of hearts? Then respond 2♥ when partner opens 1NT. Partner is required to bid the next higher ranking suit, spades in this instance.

Partner	You	♠ Q 10 8 7 5
1 NT	2 ♥	♥ K 3
2 ♠		♦ A 7 2
		♣ Q 9 2

Your hand is the same as the prior one except the heart and spade suits are switched. Here you want partner to bid spades. Following 2♥, partner must call 2♠, the next higher ranking suit.

When the opening bid is 2NT (21 to 22 points), or 2♣ followed by 2NT (23 to 24 points) the transfer procedure is the same but at one level higher on the bidding scale. When the strong partner bids 2NT, responder bids 3♦ or 3♥, requesting opener to transfer to hearts or spades respectively.

1)

Partner	You	♠ 8 6 5
2 NT	3 ♦	♥ K J 7 3 2
3 ♥	3 NT	♦ 10 9
Pass/4♥		♣ 6 5 4

This is not a very enticing hand, but prospects brighten when partner opens 2NT. Your 3♦ initiates the transfer to hearts. Partner has the final choice of 3NT or 4♥.

2)

Partner	You	♠ Q J 10 8 5
2 ♣	2 ♦	♥ 6 3
2 NT	3 ♥	♦ 9 5 2
3 ♠	3 NT	♣ 10 9 8
Pass/4♠		

Three high-card points is not a hand to brag about, but partner's 23 or 24 points are rare enough to alert you. Partner opens 2♣ (see the Two Club Convention) and follows with 2NT. Your 3♥ requests a transfer to 3♠.

Transfers are initiated by bidding diamonds or hearts following partner's 1NT or 2NT. The strong hand must respond to one of these calls by bidding the next higher suit. *Transfers guarantee a five-card suit*. A jump bid, such as 3♦ response to partner's 1NT opener, is not Stayman - this is a natural call, forcing to game.

Why Bother?

Most discussions about transfers begin by observing that a partnership is likely to gain tricks when the strong hand becomes declarer in a suit contract. There is some logic to this view. Surely your opponents are at a disadvantage when they can't see your best assets because they are hidden in the closed hand. Furthermore there is the cheerful prospect that by leading blindly into your strength at trick one, the defense may give you an otherwise unavailable trick.

Partner	You	♠ A 7 5 3 2
1 NT	2 ♥	♥ J 3
2 ♠	3 NT	♦ Q 10 3
4 ♠		♣ Q 3 2

With 9 high-card points, game in notrump or spades looks good. The first task is to get partner to call spades. The transfer achieves this efficiently. After partner complies, jump to 3NT. This way you notify partner that you have five spades and game strength. Partner likes your spades and proceeds to 4♠. This hand is South in **Deal Number 9** (see page 60), played in a world championship contest. A diamond was led up to declarer's ♦K, enabling him to take two diamond tricks and make the contract. Playing this deal at another table, the North-South pair did not transfer, playing the same 4♠ contract with South as declarer. West chose to lead a safe trump and South was unable to win a second diamond trick.

Gaining an additional trick by arranging for the strong hand to become declarer in a suit contract is not a frequent event. Less than 20% of transfers produce an extra trick, but that occasional benefit is worth the effort. There is, however, another good reason: transfers allow you to describe certain invitational hands that standard bidding cannot accommodate. These benefits are shown in some of the hands presented in the following sections.

Typically there is a price to pay when you adopt a convention, and this is so with transfers. The price here is that you lose the ability to play 2♦ contracts following 1NT openers. When you have a five-card diamond suit but are too weak to seek game, pass and play 1 NT, that is if the opposition allows it. There is little lost since 2♦ scores no better that 1NT, and only rarely does it make when 1NT does not.

Weak Hands

Here we are concerned with deals where the responder's hand is too feeble for game opposite a 1NT opener. When game is out of reach but you have a five-card major, you may pass 1NT or play in the major at the two-level. Even though your hand is anemic, generally it is preferable to play 2♥ or 2♠ rather than 1NT when you have a five-card major.

DEAL NUMBER 9

Dealer: North
Vulnerable: East/West

NORTH
♠ K Q J
♥ A 10 9
♦ K 8 4
♣ K 9 6 4

WEST
♠ 10 9 8
♥ K 6 2
♦ A J 5
♣ A 10 8 5

EAST
♠ 6 4
♥ Q 8 7 5 4
♦ 9 7 6 2
♣ J 7

SOUTH
♠ A 7 5 3 2
♥ J 3
♦ Q 10 3
♣ Q 3 2

West	North	East	South
	1 NT	Pass	2 ♥ (1)
Pass	2 ♠	Pass	3 NT
Pass	4 ♠ ///		

(1) Asking North to transfer to spades.

North opens 1NT and South calls for a transfer into spades. Having values for game, South next calls 3NT and North, with three excellent spades, proceeds to the 4♠ game.

North is the declarer and East, on lead, selects his fourth diamond. North plays low from dummy, capturing West's ♦J with the ♦K. This play promotes a second diamond trick in the dummy. Declarer counts five good spades, two diamonds, one sure club, and the ♥A, for nine tricks. He cannot get a second club unless the defense leads them first. However, if West holds one heart honor, declarer can find the tenth trick in hearts. After drawing trump, declarer leads the ♥J from dummy, leaving it ride to East's ♥Q. There is no defense; They can take their two aces but declarer will finesse hearts again for his 10th trick.

Partner	You	♠ Q 9 7 6 5
1 NT	2 ♥	♥ 4 2
2 ♠	Pass	♦ 6 5 4
		♣ K 8 5

In this series, you employ the transfer then pass. Partner becomes declarer at 2♠ where some of your spade spots become good trump tricks. You can achieve the same effect when your suit is hearts by responding 2♦, mandating a heart transfer.

Invitational Hands

When partner opens 1NT and you have 8 or 9 points, you may have game if partner has a particularly good hand of 17 or 18 points. The usual approach is to transfer then invite to game, permitting partner to make the final decision. Following the transfer, bid 2NT. This is your invitational call; there is no need to bid the five-card major as the transfer serves as this announcement.

Partner	You	♠ K 10 8 6 5
1 NT	2 ♥	♥ A 7
2 ♠	2 NT	♦ 5 4 3 2
		♣ 8 3

You have 7 high-card points and a good spade suit. If partner has extra values, the goal should be game, either 3NT or 4♠. First transfer to spades; then show the worth of your hand. Here your hand is worth a game invitation, so follow the transfer with 2NT. Now partner has four choices. With spade support, he may raise to play 3♠ or bid the spade game. Without support, he may pass to play 2NT or proceed to 3NT.

This is precision bidding, providing a dependable way to describe an invitational hand containing a five-card major. Suppose we take away the ♦2 from the above hand and make it a ♠2. This gives you six spades and 7 high-card points:

Partner	You	♠ K 10 8 6 5 2
1 NT	2 ♥	♥ A 7
2 ♠	3 ♠	♦ 5 4 3
		♣ 8 3

When partner opens 1 NT, this hand is nearly good enough for game. Follow the spade transfer with a raise to 3♠. Partner should be able to deduce that you have invitational strength and six spades, because with six spades and game strength, you would have jumped directly to 4♠.

The situation is different when partner opens 2NT. There is no room for an invitational process. You may transfer and pass, playing for part-score at the three-level, but any other positive action will find the partnership in game. But then, all you need is 4 or 5 points for a game try facing partner's 21 or 22 points.

Game Hands

It is nice to pick up a hand with abundant values and hear partner open 1NT. With 10+ points, you want to commit to game somewhere.

Partner	You	♠ Q 7 6 5 2
1 NT	2 ♥	♥ A 10 5
2 ♠	3 NT	♦ A J 8
Pass/4 ♠		♣ 5 3

First render the transfer to 2♠, advising partner of your five spades. Next bid 3NT, showing game values. Partner selects the final contract - that is 3 NT or 4♠. This is nearly an automatic choice: holding two spades, he passes 3 NT; holding three or four spades, he goes on to 4♠.

The transfer can be quite useful when you have a two-suited hand. You can show both suits, letting partner take his pick, but you need game strength to accomplish this.

Partner	You	♠ Q 9 7 6 2
1 NT	2 ♥	♥ K 10 9 8 5
2 ♠	3 ♥	♦ A 10
		♣ 9

Partner opens 1NT. This two-suiter has the values for game in notrump or either major. By transferring to spades then bidding hearts, you have described two five-card suits and game values. This gives partner three game choices, hearts, spades or notrump.

Suppose partner opens 2NT (21 to 22 points). With a five-card major, execute the transfer then raise to 3NT, leaving the final choice to partner.

	Partner	You	♠ K J 7 6 2
1)	2 NT	3 ♥	♥ 7 6 5
	3 ♠	3 NT	♦ 10 6
			♣ Q 9 8

Complete the transfer then bid 3NT. This leaves partner the final choice.

However holding a six-card major, you should play in the major rather than notrump. In these instances, complete the transfer then bid the game directly.

2)	Partner	You	♠ A 9 7 6 4 2
	2 NT	3 ♥	♥ 10 6 5
	3 ♠	4 ♠	♦ J 6
			♣ 3 2

With a six-card suit, the situation is different as partner's notrump opener assures you of a 6-2 fit. You do not need to leave the decision to partner. Intending to end in 4♠, first call for the transfer then bid the game yourself.

Exceptions

Often you have a choice as to who becomes declarer, and at times there is a good reason not to transfer.

Partner	You	♠ J 7 2
1 NT	?	♥ A J 9 8 6
		♦ 10 2
		♣ K 5 2

You have a good heart suit and 9 high-card points. If partner has three hearts, you should like to be in a heart game. There are two ways to proceed. You may employ the transfer and partner will become declarer, or you may jump to 3♥ (game-forcing, five hearts) in which case you will become declarer if partner accepts hearts.

This hand was North in board 100 played in the 1989 World Championship in Perth, Australia, where a USA team played a 176 board match against Brazil for the final championship. When the Brazilian pair played this deal, they transferred and South became declarer in a 4♥ contract as shown in **Deal Number 10** (see page 64). The contract was set two tricks as the defense started with a club lead through the dummy's ♣K. When the Americans played the same North-South hands, they arrived at the same 4♥ contract, without having transferred. The defense was unable to attack clubs at the outset and the North-South USA pair made one more trick than the Brazilians, set one but winning the board. It was not enough though as Brazil proceeded to win the championship 442 to 388.

DEAL NUMBER 10

Dealer: West
Vulnerable: All

NORTH
♠ J 7 2
♥ A J 9 8 6
♦ 10 2
♣ K J 2

WEST
♠ K 10 6
♥ Q
♦ Q 8 6 5 3
♣ 10 9 5 3

EAST
♠ 8 4 3
♥ 10 5 4 3
♦ J 7 4
♣ A Q 8

SOUTH
♠ A Q 9 5
♥ K 7 2
♦ A K 9
♣ 7 6 4

West	North	East	South
Pass	Pass	Pass	1 NT
Pass	2 ♦ (1)	Pass	2 ♥
Pass	3 NT	Pass	4 ♥ ///

(1) Asking South to transfer to hearts.

North has game values and a good heart suit and partner opens 1NT.
North orders a transfer into hearts then jumps to 3NT, giving South a
choice of 3 NT or 4♥. Having adequate heart support, South opts
for 4♥.

West leads a low club to the ♣J and East's ♣Q. In order to retain his ♣A
behind the dummy king, East switches to a low spade, partner winning with
the ♠K. Another club lead and the defense wins three club tricks and
Eventually the heart ten, for five tricks to the defense - set two tricks.

This last deal is not a random event that could just as well have turned out the other way. Here the club suit is particularly vulnerable to a lead from the right side. Holding this club suit, North should avoid the transfer in favor of a jump to 3♥ in order to be sure of becoming declarer if North continues to 4♥. The message is that when you have game strength or better, transfers should not be used automatically. Instead your first consideration should be to assess the risk of a lead from the right hand opponent.

The choice of declarer (to transfer or not) is available also when partner opens 2NT and you have a six-card suit. You may become declarer by jumping directly to game; or you may make partner declarer by using the transfer process. This decision should depend on the need to protect your kings and queens from attack by RHO.

Partner	You	
2 NT	4 ♠	♠ J 9 7 4 3 2
		♥ K 6
		♦ K 8 6
		♣ 3 2

Here you have two kings to fret over. Jump directly to 4♠ to place the contract in your hand so LHO must lead first.

Is It A Transfer?

As we have seen, the transfer can be invoked following 1NT and 2NT openers, where responses of 2♦ and 2♥ following a 1NT opener are reserved for transfers, as are 3♦ and 3♥ responses following a 2NT opener.

The transfer may be used following partner's 1NT overcall just as though partner had opened 1NT, provided of course responder has not already bid.

When the strong hand has opened 2♣ (conventional), intending to call notrump next, responder can only use the transfer after his first response was a negative 2♦. Any other call announces a good suit so there is no further use for the transfer action.

Of course there is no point in transferring after you have already had an opportunity to show a five-card major.

         *   *   *   *

Jacoby Transfers - Winning Ways

When playing the transfer convention, you may not use 2♦ or 2♥
following 1NT, or 3♦ or 3♥ following 2NT, for any other purpose.
The transfer is an automatic notice to partner that you have a five-card
major.
After partner has complied with the transfer request, you may:
- Pass and play for part-score in your suit.
- Bid 2NT to show an invitational hand.
- Bid 3NT to show game strength. Then if partner likes your major, he may
  proceed to four.

 When going for game, do not transfer if you have kings and/or queens at
risk from attack by right-hand opponent.

6
THE MAJORS

The expression "five-card majors" refers to the rule that, when the opening suit is hearts or spades, it contains at least five cards. This is a "modern" invention introduced in the nineteen-fifties, primarily by Alvin Roth and his partner Tobias Stone. While quick to take hold, it's potential advantages were not fully realized until late in the century.

When responder has three-card support, he knows the partnership has an eight-card fit and this constitutes sufficient trump for any contract. Responder is obliged to show support at his first or second bid. _As soon as a major has been supported, that suit becomes the designated trump_.

It is apparent that, short of slam appeal, when your partnership has earned a partial score toward game, you should continue bidding only as far as needed to complete the game. This may mean passing the opening bid or stopping at the two-level or three-level, whatever it takes. For the most part, responses and rebids discussed in this chapter presume the partnership does not have a part-score, thus needs 100 points for game.

OPENING BIDS

With a five-card major and 13 to 20 points, open 1♥ or 1♠ unless the hand qualifies to open 1NT.

1) ♠ K Q 8 7 4   With 12 high-card points, this is a
    ♥ K 4   typical minimum opener.
    ♦ A 9 3 2
    ♣ 10 3

2)   ♠ A K 10 7 6   This hand has 20 points, about the upper
        ♥ 7   limit for a one-level opener.
        ♦ A Q 4
        ♣ K Q 9 3

3)   ♠ A 7   You have 18 high-card points. You may
        ♥ J 8 7 5 4   open 1♥ but 1NT is preferred.
        ♦ A Q J
        ♣ K Q J 3

4)   ♠ J 4   This hand is too strong to open 1NT. Open
        ♥ K Q J 5 4   1♥; if partner says 1♠, jump to 2NT,
        ♦ A Q 7   showing a balanced 19 or 20 points.
        ♣ K J 10

Two-suited hands are more challenging. With minimal opening values, favor the higher-ranked suit because it can be troublesome or impossible to show the second suit later. Strong hands (17 points or more) allow you more flexibility because you have the option of opening the lower-ranked suit then reversing into the higher-ranked suit at the second bid.

1)   ♠ K Q 9 6 5   If you open 1♦, you will be unable to
        ♥ K 2   convince partner that you have five spades.
        ♦ A 10 9 7 5   Open 1♠. If partner responds 2♣, you may
        ♣ Q   show your diamonds without raising the ante.

2)   ♠ K Q J 10 7   With this so-so hand, open ♠. If partner
        ♥ Q 5   responds 2♦ or 2♥, rebid spades, even
        ♦ 8   though this unsupported rebid suggests a
        ♣ K 6 5 3 2   six-card suit. The hand is too weak to bid
                              clubs at the three-level.

3)   ♠ A Q J 10 5   Certainly you are strong enough to open 1♠
        ♥ K 8   and rebid 3♦, a jump shift, over most any
        ♦ A K 8 7 6   call partner chooses.
        ♣ 4

SINGLE RAISES

When your partner opens, you have an obligation to respond with 6 points, otherwise there is the prospect of missing game. A minimal response (6 to 9 points, possibly 10 in a pinch) is worth one free bid. Having support, the best use of that one bid is to raise partner's major to the two-level. This raise establishes trump and simultaneously defines your limitations.

Partner	You	♠ K 10 9 8 5
1 ♥	2 ♥	♥ 9 8 5
		♦ K 4 3
		♣ 7 5

> You have 7 points, three hearts and five spades. It may be tempting to bid spades, but resist the impulse. This hand is worth only one free bid.

The range of a single raise encompasses a four point spread, which may seem rather broad, but is quite manageable because there remains an entire level of bidding below game to sort out the weak from the strong.

Opener's Second Bid

Suppose you open the bidding with 1♠ and partner raises to 2♠. You having three choices - pass, invite to game, or jump directly to game. The decision of course depends on your strength. If you have less than 17 points, the partnership has 22 to 25 points - not quite enough for game so you may pass. If you have more than 19 points the decision is easy because the partnership is assured of 26 points.

♠ A K 7 6 5	You	Partner
♥ 8	1 ♠	2 ♠
♦ A Q 8 6	4 ♠	
♣ K Q 6		

> With 18 high-card points and a singleton, you have enough here to contract for the game.

Our main concern is what to do with hands of 17 to 18 points because it is not yet clear whether the partnership has game values. Does partner have a minimum (6 to 7) or maximum (8 to 9)? It is fundamental that any further bid by you after partner's raise, if not forcing is an invitation to game. To invite to game, you may rebid your major at the three level.

♠ K J 6 4 3	You	Partner
♥ 7 4 2	1 ♠	2 ♠
♦ A K Q	3 ♠	
♣ A 7		

With 18 points, you are on the verge of game. Your 3♠ bid is a direct game invitation. If partner has 8 or 9 points, you have a good shot at a game.

Trial Bids

You can refine the invitational process and perhaps gain an edge over the opposition with the trial bid. Suppose you open 1♥ with a hand valued at 17 to 19 points. Partner gives you a single raise to 2♥. You may have a game if partner has more than a minimum so you issue an invitation. When you bid a new suit you promise a queen or better and a suit of three cards or more. When responder has an honor in this secondary suit, the combined assets increase in value.

1)	*West*	*East*	*West*	*East*
	♠ A K 9 7 6	♠ Q 8 3	1 ♠	2 ♠
	♥ 10	♥ K J 7	3 ♣	3 ♠
	♦ A Q 8 3	♦ J 10 4		
	♣ Q 7 6	♣ 8 4 3 2		

West invites to game with a 3♣ bid, looking for help in clubs. With a minimum 7 points, a flat hand, and no club honor, East signs off at 3♠. In the play of the hand, West should take five spades and three diamonds most of the time. If the ♦K and ♥A are favorably placed, perhaps two more tricks could be found and game made. However the odds of taking 10 tricks are rather poor, about 1 in 4.

2)	*West*	*East*	*West*	*East*
	♠ A K 9 7 6	♠ Q 8 3	1 ♠	2 ♠
	♥ 10	♥ 8 4 3 2	3 ♣	4 ♠
	♦ A Q 8 3	♦ J 10 4		
	♣ Q 7 6	♣ K J 7		

Here are the same hands as in example 1 except that the hearts and clubs are switched in East's hand. Now when West invites with his 3♣ bid, East should be pleased enough to upgrade his hand and jump to 4♠. In the play, West can expect to take five spades, three or four diamonds, and two clubs.

The key to success with the trial bid is for the opener to select a suit that has intermediate honors that are enhanced in value if partner has an honor or two in the same suit. Typical trial suits have holdings such as Q-x-x, K-x-x, K-J-x, and A-J-x, and may contain a fourth card. Each of these combinations increase in value when partner has an ace, king or queen to complement opener's values.

Responder has the final decision. If he has maximum values (8 or 9 points) after re-valuing his assets in light of the trial bid, he should continue to game, otherwise sign off at three of partner's suit.

JUMP RAISES

If you are good enough to contract for nine tricks, bid them. When you have 11or 12 dummy points and support for partner's major, you are a tad away from game, certainly good enough to send partner an invitational message. Here the message is sent on the wings of the jump raise.

Partner	You	♠ 9 8 7 5
1 ♠	3 ♠	♥ K 4
		♦ K Q 8 7 4
		♣ 6 5

When partner opens 1♠ your hand is worth 11 dummy points. Stay mum about your diamonds. You already have a golden fit in spades and there's no sense in alerting opponents that you have good diamonds.

As has already been noted the 10-point hand is a bit too weak to play for nine tricks opposite a minimum opener. The larger problem, however, is that if you raise 1♥ to 3♥ or 1♠ to 3♠ with 10 to 12 points, partner must make a game decision without knowing whether you have a minimum 10 points or a maximum 12 points. There is no bidding space left to discover more about your hand. If he has 14 or 15 points, he will be short of game if you have only 10. These same hands are good bets if you have 11 or 12 points. As responder, you make life easier for partner by evaluating your hand more precisely - is it a good 10-pointer or a poor one? If the hand has no extra attractions, make a single raise instead of a jump raise.

1)	Partner	You	♠ 8 4 3
	1 ♥	3 ♥	♥ K 10 8
			♦ K Q J 8
			♣ 7 5

There are no wasted honors - great trump support and a solid diamond honor sequence, money in the bank. This hand warrants a jump to 3♥.

2)   *Partner*   *You*   ♠ J 9 8
          1 ♥   2 ♥   ♥ Q 7 2
                                          ♦ K 5 2
                                          ♣ A 10 5 4

Honors are unsupported and distribution flat. This hand is worth only a
single raise.

Opener's Second Bid

Partner has given you a jump raise, defining his hand as 11 to 12
points. It is apparent that if you, the opener, have a little extra, about 15
points, you ought to go for the game. But with a minimum, pass and play
for the part-score.

1)   ♠ A K 8 7 6   *You*   *Partner*
          ♥ 10 9   1 ♠   3 ♠
          ♦ A J 5   Pass
          ♣ 7 5 4

This hand is a minimum opener - 12 high-card points, 1 for distribution,
and no good side suit and no well-placed intermediate cards. The
partnership's combined values total 24 or 25 points.

2)   ♠ A K 4   *You*   *Partner*
          ♥ A Q J 9 7   1 ♥   3 ♥
          ♦ 6 5   4 ♥
          ♣ 6 4 3

You have 15 points and all honors are working. Therefore partnership
assets are ample for a game try. This is an easy call.

3)   ♠ A 9   *You*   *Partner*
          ♥ A K Q 7 6   1 ♥   3 ♥
          ♦ 7 2   4 ♣
          ♣ K Q J 4

Add partner's 11 points to your 21 and you are in slam range, but the
diamond suit could be an Achilles heal. Here your 4♣ bid shows a key
control in that suit and slam interest (otherwise you would go directly to
4♥). Hopefully partner will answer with a 4♦ bid.

GAME RAISES

As we have seen, a jump raise to the three-level requires 11 to 12 points, just short of game values. It is a logical extension to jump one level higher, to game, with a supporting hand of 13 to 14 points.

Traditionally this double-jump raise was seen as rich in trump, unbalanced, and weak in honors. This narrow definition required unnecessarily complicated treatments for other balanced, game-strength hands. With today's more accurate evaluation of unbalanced hands, all supporting 13 or 14 point hands, distributional or not, are included in the double-jump raise. Further discussion of this modern double-jump raise is presented in **NOTE 2: Major Suits - Jump Raises to Game**, page 204.

Partner opens a major, and you have support for that major in a hand worth 13 or 14 dummy points. There is little reason to respond in a new suit as you already have a good major suit fit, and there is no reason to tell the opposition about an attractive side suit. After a simple addition, you know that the partnership has 26 points, and that gets you to a major-suit game.

1)   *Partner*   *You*   ♠ J 10 5 6 2
        1 ♠   4 ♠   ♥ K 9 4 3
                                     ♦ A 9 4
                                     ♣ 6

You are weak in honors but long in trump support. The distribution points of the short club suit and the extra heart support create sufficient value for the game jump.

2)   *Partner*   *You*   ♠ Q 10 5
        1 ♠   4 ♠   ♥ K 5
                                     ♦ Q 9 6 5 3
                                     ♣ A Q 6

You have spade support and 13 high-card points, just right to contract for 10 tricks.

3)   *Partner*   *You*   ♠ J 6 2
        1 ♠   4 ♠   ♥ A 9 4 3
                                     ♦ A 10 9 6
                                     ♣ K 6

This hand has 12 very good high-card points, good intermediate values, and spade support. It is worth a game raise. Your hand is South in **Deal Number 11** (see page 74).

DEAL NUMBER 11

Dealer: West
Vulnerable: East-West

NORTH
♠ A K Q 9 7
♥ 8
♦ K Q 5
♣ 10 9 7 2

WEST
♠ 10 8 4 3
♥ K J 5
♦ J 8 7 4
♣ A 4

EAST
♠ 5
♥ Q 10 7 6 2
♦ 3 2
♣ Q J 8 5 3

SOUTH
♠ J 6 2
♥ A 9 4 3
♦ A 10 9 6
♣ K 6

West	North	East	South
Pass	1 ♠	Pass	4 ♠ ///

South has 12 good high-card points and the short clubs might be worth another point. Valuing his hand at 13 points, he raises to game.

East leads the ♣Q to dummy's king and West's ace. West returns with the ♣4, looking very much like a doubleton club holding. Declarer counts 5 spades, 1 heart, 3 diamonds. The fourth diamond may produce a trick if the jack falls. In clubs, declarer has the 10-9 and only the jack is outstanding. He plays the ♣9 on the second trick, taken by East's ♣J. East plays a third club, South discarding a heart and West ruffing. Not wanting to lead away from his heart or diamond honors, West leads trump, North winning with the ace. At this point there are only two trump outstanding, so declarer leads the fourth club, ruffing with dummy's ♠J. Declarer no longer needs to take a fourth diamond trick as he now can account for 10 tricks - 5 spades, 1 heart, 3 diamonds, and 1 club ruff in dummy.

INDIRECT JUMP RAISES

Direct raises define supporting hands of 6 points to 14 points. With stronger hands, having slam possibilities when partner opens the bidding, it is appropriate to go slower and exchange more information along the way. With 15 or 16 points, the approach is to respond in a new suit then show support by a raise to game.

Partner	You	
1 ♠	2 ♣	♠ Q 3 2
		♥ A Q J
		♦ 9 6 4
		♣ A Q 7 2

Your hand is worth 15 points in support of spades. Now is the time to call a new suit as the first of two steps. Bid 2♣, intending next to jump to 4♠.

Responder's Second Bid

Your second bid completes the description of a strong, supporting hand by means of the game raise.

Partner	You	
1 ♠	2 ♣	♠ Q 10 4
2 ♦	4 ♠	♥ A Q 6
		♦ 9 4
		♣ A Q 8 5 4

In addition to having defined your values with some precision, partner is advised of your spade support and club values. He is fully armed to evaluate slam prospects.

An alternate scenario arises when partner makes a strong rebid. Now you no longer need to finish describing your hand; you know the combined strength and it becomes your responsibility to pursue slam.

Partner	You	
1 ♥	2 ♦	♠ J 10 9 3
2 ♠	4 NT	♥ K 4 2
		♦ K Q J 6
		♣ A 6

Partner's reverse promises 17 points or so, giving the partnership 32 points. Partner does not need to know you have heart support; nor does he need to know your strength, although he should be able to work it out. The final contract is yours to select. The 4NT bid is Blackwood.

JUMP SHIFTS

Responder's game-forcing jump shift is employed with hands of 17 or 18 points. When you have support, jump shift then follow with a raise.

1)   *Partner*   *You*   ♠ Q J 8
      1 ♠   3 ♦   ♥ 7
                                ♦ A Q 8 7 6
                                ♣ A Q 6 2

You have 17 points in support of spades. Jump to 3♦ to define this big hand. Whatever partner does next, steer the contract into spades.

2)   *Partner*   *You*   ♠ Q J 9 6
      1 ♠   3 ♣   ♥ J 4 3
                                ♦ A Q J
                                ♣ A Q 4

Normally the jump shift promises a four-card suit, but with a flat hand, you may still jump to show strength. This does not present a problem because the final contract is going to be spades.

Opener's Second Bid

Responder makes a jump shift. When you do not know where the auction is headed, select a natural bid at the lowest level, even though you may be strong enough for slam.

      ♠ A 9   *You*   *Partner*
      ♥ A K Q 4 3   1 ♥   3 ♣
      ♦ Q 6 5 4   3 ♦
      ♣ 8 6

You have a good 16-point opening bid and partner's response shows 17 points. You are on the way to a slam but where is the question. Bid your diamonds and await more information from partner. If you have no second suit, rebid the major or notrump. There is no need to jump the bidding as partner's bid is a game force.

Responder's Second Bid

We are concerned here with strong hands that support partner's opener. At the second turn to bid, after your jump shift, you must show support. After that it will be up to partner to place the contract.

Partner	You	♠ Q J 9 8
1 ♠	3 ♣	♥ J 8 4
3 NT	4 ♠	♦ A Q J
		♣ A Q 4

The 3♣ bid defines your strength, then the spade raise sets the trump. There is no need to worry about missing slam. Partner now knows of your strength and support, and (presumably) can add as well as you.

SIX-CARD SUITS

Basic bidding rules remain intact when opener's suit contains six cards instead of five and responder has three. However some of these occasions will find responder with two-card support. A 6-2 fit is ample to provide a viable trump suit. The key to success here is for the opener to rebid his six-card suit. While at times there is no good alternative to rebidding a five-card suit, responder should assume the rebid of an unsupported major suit promises six. This makes it imperative for the opener to have a very good suit when he rebids one of only five cards.

1)

Partner	You	♠ K J 9 8
1 ♥	1 ♠	♥ J 4
2 ♥	Pass	♦ Q 10 8 7
		♣ 7 4 3

You have a modest hand, but it requires a response. In the absence of three-card support, bid spades. Partner rebids hearts and now your two hearts are sufficient. Even so, this hand is minimal and it is a good time to pass and play for a part-score.

2)

Partner	You	♠ A 9 7 6
1 ♥	1 ♠	♥ 10 5
2 ♥	3 ♥	♦ A K 10 8 7
		♣ 6 5

With but two hearts, the short club suit does not qualify for distribution points. You have a nice 11 high-card hand. When partner rebids his hearts assume he has six of them. Game remains a possibility if partner has just a little more than promised.

3)

Partner	You	♠ K Q J 7
1 ♥	1 ♠	♥ J 5
2 ♥	4 ♥	♦ A K 10 8 7
		♣ 6 5

This hand is nearly the same as the previous one, but with two more honor points, giving you game strength. The problem of where to play is solved when partner rebids his heart suit.

When opener is better than minimum, his most likely rebid is a jump in his six-card major. This assures that his major is of good quality, and that he has 17 or 18 points.

OPENER JUMPS IN NOTRUMP

Of course you must have more than a minimum opener to consider a second round jump bid. When you open a major with 17 or 18 points (plus 2 potential points for a qualifying suit), you may jump to 2NT when partner responds 1♠ to your 1♥ opener (a one-over-one response), showing 19 or 20 points. With more strength, jump to 3NT.

1)	♠ A 9	You	Partner
	♥ K Q 10 6 5	1 ♥	1 ♠
	♦ Q 8 4	2 NT	
	♣ A Q 4		

This 2NT jump bid shows balance, five hearts, stoppers in the unbid suits, and 19 to 20 points in support of notrump. If partner has more than a minimum, he should continue to game. This is the South hand in *Deal Number 12* where North continues to 3NT (see page 79). In the play of the hand, South makes an overtrick.

2)	♠ 4 3	You	Partner
	♥ A K 5 3 2	1 ♥	1 ♠
	♦ A K 8	3 NT	
	♣ K Q J		

This double jump to 3NT shows better than 20 points. This hand would qualify to open 2NT but the poor spades makes the heart opener safer. This game jump does not preclude partner going on to a major suit game or a slam.

After you open a major, often partner responds in a new suit at the two-level. This of course requires a stronger hand, at least 10 points. Now 16 points in your hand is game strength and you may bid it directly. This jump promises 16 to 18 points but may be made with 19 points when you have no other satisfactory choice.

DEAL NUMBER 12

Dealer: East
Vulnerable: East-West

NORTH
♠ K J 8 3
♥ 3 2
♦ K 5 2
♣ K 10 7 2

WEST
♠ 7 6 4
♥ 9 7 4
♦ A 7 6
♣ Q 5 4 3

EAST
♠ 10 5 2
♥ A Q 8
♦ J 10 9 3
♣ J 9 6

SOUTH
♠ A Q 9
♥ K J 10 6 5
♦ Q 8 4
♣ A 8

West	North	East	South
		Pass	1 ♥
Pass	1 ♠	Pass	2 NT
Pass	3 NT ///		

South opens 1♥. Lacking heart support, North responds 1♠ and South jumps to 2NT, asking partner to go on to game with some-thing better than a minimum, an invitation that North readily accepts.

West leads his fourth best club. Declarer plays low from dummy and captures East's ♣9 with the ♣A. He counts four spades, one diamond, and two clubs, thus needing to find two heart tricks. This is not going to be easy. He must get to dummy twice to finesse hearts. Using diamonds or clubs to get to dummy could result in losing control of one of these suits. So declarer decides to use spades, even at the risk of losing a spade trick. He leads the ♠9 to the ♠J, then returns a heart to his ♥10, East playing low (apparently East has the ♥A and ♥Q). Back to the dummy via a spade, ♠Q To ♠K. Then declarer leads another heart to East's ace, who returns a club to dummy's king. Returning to his hand via the ♠A, declarer plays his ♥K and the hearts break 3-3. Declarer wins four heart tricks, making an over-trick.

♠ K 5   *You*   *Partner*
♥ A 8 6 5 2   1 ♥   2 ♣
♦ A Q 7 5   3 NT
♣ K 6

Here you open the major with 16 high-card points rather than notrump because your distribution (5-4-2-2) is not balanced. Partner promises 10 points so you have adequate strength for a notrump game.

*   *   *   *

The Majors - Winning Ways

OPENING PARTNER:
Open 1NT rather than a major holding a balanced hand (5-3-3-2), the five-card suit being a major, and 16 to 18 points.
After opening a major, use jump bids or reverse bids to show strength beyond minimum openers.

RESPONDING PARTNER:
When you have support for an opening major and modest to intermediate strength, show your support immediately:
  • Raise with 6 to 9 points.
  • Jump raise with 11 to 12 points.
  • Raise to game with 13 to 14 points.
When you have support and great playing strength, show your support indirectly:
  • Bid a new suit then raise to game with 15 to 16 points.
  • Jump shift then raise with 17 to 18 points.
  • Approach slam via any forcing sequence with 19+ points.

7

THE MINORS

By exploiting five-card majors to the maximum, we have made a giant step toward precision bidding. The minors are more problematic, and they tend to be neglected in favor of majors and notrump. There is good reason for this state of affairs. Minors are advantageous over other strains only where they produce games and slams that cannot be made elsewhere. Of course the underlying reason that minors are second fiddle is the meager 20-point worth for each trick.

At part-score contracts, it does not matter much if the minors are neglected so long as you make the contract. Favoring notrump over a minor is a perfectly good tactic because, for instance, the difference between a nine-trick minor contract and a seven-trick notrump contract is only 20 points, and this in rubber bridge is hardly consequential. The practice of bidding up the line to explore the majors before settling in a minor is sound practice.

When you have game potential, be on the lookout for the occasional deal where the only viable contract is a minor, particularly when you do not have stoppers in all four suits, making notrump a risky choice. Otherwise only rarely does a 5♣ or 5♦ contract turn out better than 3NT. Furthermore, do not overlook the fact that *holding a good five-card minor is of considerable worth in notrump*. Consequently the first focus, with or without a five-card minor, is to determine if there is a 4-4 major fit or a balanced notrump fit. When neither of these conditions are present, a nine-card or better minor fit provides a good fall-back position.

Only when the partnership strength approaches 32 points does it need to be especially alert to a 5-3 or better minor, so that after a one-level opening, slam interests arise only when the responder has at least 12 points. When the opener has five of a minor and responder has but three or four of that suit, the process is a bit subtle. During the bidding process, if slam is possible the opener has to find a way to communicate that his minor contains at least five cards. One way to do this is to rebid

81

the suit. More often the opener calls a second suit in a context which suggests five cards in the first-bid suit and four in the second.

OPENING BIDS AND REBIDS

Absent a five-card major or a suitable notrump opener, you are compelled to open a minor. This is an easy decision when holding a suit of five or six cards. But often you have to open a four-card minor because the hand lacks a five-card suit. There are just three possible distributions that have no five-card suit. They are 4-4-3-2, 4-3-3-3, and 4-4-4-1. In the first two of these, when the four-card suits are majors, you are faced with the prospect of opening a three-card minor. Always prefer a three-card suit over a two-card suit. Hopefully in the subsequent bidding confusion no one will notice it's lack of stature. The news is not all bad though, because when you open a diamond, 95% of the time it's length will be at least four. Consequently when partner opens 1♦, it is a very good bet that it contains four cards and perhaps more. The club suit is not quite so accommodating, but still the odds are well in favor of finding four, about 85% of the time. In view of these statistics, it seems reasonable to assume that when partner opens a minor, he has four of them. The challenge is to find 5-4 fits that play better in the minor than in some other strain, notrump in particular.

You may open a minor with 13 to 20+ points. However *when your hand qualifies for notrump, open 1NT rather than a minor*.

_Four-Card Minors

Open the longer minor when you do not have a five-card major or a notrump opener. Absent a five-card minor, open diamonds when the minors are 4-4 and clubs when they are 3-3. You can readily find a major suit fit if there is one, or otherwise settle into a respectable notrump contract.

1)	♠ A 8 7 6	This four-card diamond suit is the
	♥ 7 3	standard opener. Even so, the most
	♦ Q J 10 7	likely prospects to play are spades
	♣ A Q 2	or notrump.

2) ♠ K Q 7 4   Yes, you should open 1♣. If partner has
    ♥ Q 10 7 6   so little that he can not respond, then the
    ♦ A 4   opposition will certainly compete, most
    ♣ Q 8 5   likely to game.

3) ♠ A Q 6 5   Open diamonds. With 19 high-card points
    ♥ K 8   this hand is too strong to open 1NT.
    ♦ Q J 10 4
    ♣ A K 3

Five-Card Minors

When you open a minor, partner assumes it contains four cards. At times you want to let partner know it is longer, especially when the hand is strong or when partner responds in a way that suggests slam potential. There are several ways to show a five-card minor.

1) ♠ 8 4 3   *You*   *Partner*
    ♥ 10 4   1 ♦   1 ♠
    ♦ K Q J 10 3   2 ♦
    ♣ A Q 8

Note here a key difference between minors and majors. Your rebid of a major ordinarily shows a six-card suit whereas the minor rebid shows a good five-card suit.

2) ♠ Q J 7   *You*   *Partner*
    ♥ 3 2   1 ♦   1 ♠
    ♦ K Q J 10 7 6   3 ♦
    ♣ A Q

This strong hand with it's excellent diamonds warrants an unsupported jump rebid. A heart call by partner will lead to a notrump game; a spade rebid should prompt you to raise to 4♠.

3) ♠ K 8   *You*   *Partner*
    ♥ 10 9   1 ♦   1 ♠
    ♦ K Q 7 5 4   2 ♣
    ♣ A Q 9 6

Open the longer minor. Normally your second suit contains four cards, implying five in the first suit. Consequently this 1♦ - - 2♣ sequence advises partner of five diamonds and four clubs, and of course shortness in the majors. Being able to read all of the inferences inherent in each bidding sequence is a talent that should be cultivated.

4)   ♠ 7   *You*   *Partner*
       ♥ K Q 5 3   1 ♦   1 ♠
       ♦ A K 9 6 4   2 ♥
       ♣ K Q 10

Open 1♦ then bid hearts next. This reverse promises a strong hand with five clubs and four hearts, and at least 17 points. This hand also is good enough to jump to 2NT over partner's 1♠, but the heart call is descriptive and allows partner to bid notrump first if he wishes.

5)   ♠ K Q J 8   *You*   *Partner*
       ♥ K Q   1 ♦   1 ♥
       ♦ A Q J 9 6   2 ♠
       ♣ 9 5

Of course bidding spades at one level higher than necessary is a jump shift. Additionally it implies five diamonds and four spades.

FIRST AND SECOND RESPONSES

Initial responses to minor suit openings are based on the premise that partner is bidding a four-card suit. Subsequent bidding may show it to be longer, but meanwhile that is the appropriate assumption. Whille a 4-4 fit is deemed an adequate trump holding, do not be too eager to confirm a 4-4 fit in a minor suit.

You should be alert to possible 4-4 major fits; and to that end, standard practice is to show a four-card major immediately following partner's minor opening. By doing this, you will always find a 4-4 major if the partnership has one. In the event you have four cards in both majors, bid hearts first, enabling partner to immediately show a four-card spade suit when he has one.

With Support For Partner's Minor

It is usually correct to respond in your four-card majors up the line while having support for partner's minor. This practice contrasts with major-suit bidding where your usual action is to show support immediately. Here you delay showing such support unless there seems to be no other useful line of inquiry.

Delayed Raises

Partner opens a minor. Respond in your four-card or longer major first then show your minor suit support later if it is appropriate to do so - a delayed raise would be proper and descriptive at the second round of bidding if you have not found a major fit or a viable notrump prospect.

Delayed raises in the minors operate in a different context than in the majors where a response in a new suit followed by a jump raise shows 15 to 16 points. Alternatively, after a minor opening, your purpose for calling a new suit is to test for a major; and you may later show support by a delayed raise or jump raise, keeping in mind that a minor-suit game requires eleven tricks, 29 points. A delayed jump to the three-level indicates 13 or 14 points (invitational), and to game, 15 or 16 points.

	Partner	*You*	
1)			♠ 8 4 3 2
	1 ♦	1 ♥	♥ A K 8 5
	2 ♣	2 ♦	♦ 8 7 5
			♣ 10 4

You have 7 points and some diamond support. Here your delayed raise shows nothing more than a preference for partner's diamonds.

	Partner	*You*	
2)			♠ 6
	1 ♦	1 ♥	♥ K 8 6 4
	1 NT	3 ♦	♦ K 7 5 3 2
			♣ K J 4

This sequence enables you to test the heart suit then jump raise to show a strong hand and good support.

	Partner	*You*	
3)			♠ 8 3
	1 ♦	1 ♥	♥ K Q 5 4
	2 ♠	3 ♦	♦ J 10 7 5
			♣ 6 5 3

This is not a notable hand but partner forces. The diamond raise is descriptive and allows the strong hand to declare notrump if appropriate.

	Partner	*You*	
4)			♠ 6
	1 ♦	1 ♥	♥ K 5 4 3
	1 ♠	5 ♦	♦ Q J 10 3 2
			♣ A Q 2

Partner's spade bid does not suggest slam values so you may as well close out at game. This hand is North in ***Deal Number 13*** (see page 86).

DEAL NUMBER 13

Dealer: South
Vulnerable: None

NORTH
♠ 6
♥ K 5 4 3
♦ Q J 10 3 2
♣ A Q 2

WEST
♠ K Q 7
♥ 9 7 6 2
♦ 7
♣ J 10 6 5 3

EAST
♠ J 9 5 4 2
♥ A 10
♦ A 9 6
♣ 8 7 4

SOUTH
♠ A 10 8 3
♥ Q J 8
♦ K 8 5 4
♣ K 9

West	North	East	South
			1 ♦
Pass	1 ♥	Pass	1 ♠
Pass	5 ♦ ///		

Holding a minimum, South opens 1♦. North counts 12 high-card points
and 4 distribution points (singleton and the fifth diamond). He is strong
enough to insist on game, presumably in 5♦. But first he bids 1♥ to give
the partnership time to find the best contract. South's second bid does not
offer any slam values so North jumps to the game in diamonds.

On a club lead, South sees 10 tricks (3 clubs, 4 diamonds, 2 hearts and
1 spade) after driving out the two missing aces. He begins by taking
the ♣K in hand and driving out the trump ace. East switches to a spade,
taken with the ♠A in his hand. Declarer clears trump and plays hearts
to East's ♥A. There is no defense as South ruffs the fourth heart for the
11th trick, losing only the two aces.

5)   *Partner*   *You*   ♠ A Q 9 7
        1 ♣   2 ♠   ♥ 7 6
        2 NT   3 ♣   ♦ A 4
                                       ♣ A J 9 3 2

This hand qualifies for a game-forcing jump shift. Apparently partner
cannot raise spades or rebid clubs so he settles on 2NT. This deal has
distinct possibilities of a club slam. Having advised partner of your
considerable strength, a 3♣ bid now paints a substantive picture of your
hand.

Immediate Raises

There are some hands where an immediate raise is preferred over
a new suit or notrump. These are hands that are long in partner's minor
and without a four-card major. You may raise with four-card support or
better.

1)   *Partner*   *You*   ♠ 6 5 2
        1 ♣   2 ♣   ♥ 9 8 7
                                       ♦ Q 8 4
                                       ♣ K J 10 5

You have a minimum hand and little to offer except club support. A 2♣
response is descriptive. It declares a minimum hand, club support, and
absence of a four-card major.

2)   *Partner*   *You*   ♠ 10 9
        1 ♦   3 ♦   ♥ A 7 5
                                       ♦ K Q 6 5 4
                                       ♣ 8 3 2

The fifth diamond is worth 2 points, making a total of 12. Your jump raise
indicates good support, invitational strength, and nothing else to suggest.

Without Support For Partner's Minor

Not having support for partner's minor, you must search for a
satisfactory strain, being careful not to push the bidding too high. First try
your four-card (or better) major. If there is a 4-4 major, you will find it
promptly. If not, notrump is the back-up, unless of course partner has a
long/strong minor and persists in rebidding it.

1)   *Partner*   *You*   ♠ K J 8
        1 ♣   1 ♥   ♥ A 10 7 6
        2 ♥   Pass   ♦ 9 7 6 4
                                       ♣ 7 6

Show your four hearts, which partner promptly raises. Now you have
found a 4-4 major. Partner's raise does not promise any more than
minimal values, thus the partnership is well short of game.

2)   *Partner*   *You*   ♠ A J 7 6 5
        1 ♣   1 ♠   ♥ 8 5 3
        2 NT   3 ♠   ♦ 8 2
                                     ♣ Q 6 5

Partner jumps to 2NT after you show your spade suit. The 2NT jump
defines a balanced hand with 19 or 20 points. Game is definitely in the
cards. If partner has 3 spades, the contract may play better in spades
than in notrump. Rebid spades to inform partner that it is a five-card suit.

3)   *Partner*   *You*   ♠ Q 10 9
        1 ♣   1 ♥   ♥ A 9 6 5
        1 NT   Pass   ♦ K 7 5
                                     ♣ 6 4 2

This 1NT denies four of either major, and suggests a minimum 13 to 15
points. At this stage, notrump is the obvious choice. Since there is no
game in sight, pass; but if you have a partial score and need just a little
more than 40 points for game, then by all means raise to 2NT.

4)   *Partner*   *You*   ♠ 10 9 3 2
        1 ♣   1 ♥   ♥ K Q 3 2
        2 ♣   2 NT   ♦ A J 10
                                     ♣ Q 8

Your hand contains 12 high-card points, sufficient for a 2NT call.
However notrump can wait. Try for a major suit fit first then bid notrump
if there is no fit.

5)   *Partner*   *You*   ♠ K 7 6 5
        1 ♦   1 ♠   ♥ 10 8
        2 ♥   3 NT   ♦ K 9 7
                                     ♣ K 10 4 3

Partner reverses. You have 9 high-card points and support for
diamonds. In some circumstances a second bid of 3♣ would be
desirable, allowing partner another opportunity to further describe his
hand or to declare in 3NT. Not here. With this particular hand it is better
for you to become declarer to protect your kings from attack by RHO.

Bidding a Second New Suit

There are but few situations where it is useful for the responder to
bid a second new suit (forcing). You will not find a 4-4 fit in your second
suit, so the implications are: you have more strength (at least invitational)

than indicated by your first response; and your first suit is at least five cards in length.

Partner	You	
		♠ 6 3
1 ♦	1 ♥	♥ A Q 9 8 7
1 NT	2 ♣	♦ 8
		♣ A K 4 3 2

This is a strong hand and you would like to find a game contract. Partner has a balanced hand and surely has some heart or club support.

*   *   *   *

The Minors - Winning Ways

With 5-3-3-2 distribution including a five-card minor, open 1NT whenever you have 16 to 18 points
When you cannot open a five-card major or notrump, open the longest minor, or:
- With 4-4 or longer in the minors, open diamonds.
- With 3-3 in the minors, open clubs.

To show a five-card minor:
- Rebid the minor.
- Bid a new suit (implying the first suit is five)

Continue bidding minors only when the hand:
- Shows no promise for notrump or a major.
- Has slam potential in the minor.

8
THE TWO CLUB CONVENTION

Most biddable hands are opened at the one-level, providing maximum space to explore possibilities of game and slam. There are some hands, however, that are so strong that game is possible even when partner is too weak to respond to a one-level opener. In these situations you need a way to force partner to keep the bidding alive. The solution is to open with a 2♣ call, which is purely conventional and absolutely forcing. This is a modern invention. In earlier days, such hands were opened with a natural suit bid at the two-level; but now we have a much better use for 2♦, 2♥ and 2♠ openers.

For unbalanced hands, the 2♣ call is followed by naming your strong suit at the next round of bidding. A typical sequence is:

You	*Partner*	This two-step process describes a
2♣	2♦	strong unbalanced hand with a very
2♥		good heart suit.

Usually you can name your major suit at the two-level; but when it is a minor, partner's required response sometimes prevents you from identifying it at the two level, so your second bid then must be 3♣ or 3♦.

One might fairly wonder: why employ an artificial bid when a natural one is available? The advantages of this convention do not readily jump out at you because they accrue indirectly. Using the 2♣ opener for most strong hands allows 2♦, 2♥, and 2♠ openers to represent weak distributional hands (see Chapter 9: Weak Two Openers). The key point is that these weak hands occur twenty times as often as the strong hands; and now we have the means to effectively compete with both types. Competing with weak distributional hands is a major gain in the art of bidding, and is the primary justification for adopting this convention. There is another substantial benefit that accrues from this convention. The 2♣ opener is used also to describe strong balanced hands of 23 points and higher. This application enables tighten the notrump bidding structure for all hands stronger than 18 points into ranges of 2 points.

UNBALANCED HANDS

Responder may pass a one-level opener when he has less than six points, and opener then plays a part-score contract, unless of course the opponents decide to contest. This consequence is quite acceptable except in situations where games can be made even when partner has less than six points. From a count point-of-view, if you have less than 21 points, game is not likely unless partner has 6 points. Games are not lost when you open at the one-level with less than 21 points because partner will respond positively with 6 points to keep the bidding alive. On the other hand, when you exceed 20 points and want to be sure of a response, you must do something exceptional - and that is to open 2♣. Partner must respond and game is sought whenever responder can contribute a few significant points.

Opening Bids

The 2♣ opener makes no promise as to the club suit. Presumably it promises an unbalanced hand worth at least 8 1/2 tricks or 21 plus points and a very good as yet unnamed suit, a solid five or good six in length. The distinction between an unbalanced and balanced hand will be clarified when the opener makes his second bid.

1)   ♠ K Q 6   This hand is so strong that game can be
        ♥ A K Q 6 4 3   made with nothing more than the spade
        ♦ A K 9 2   jack in partner's hand. Open 2♣ and
        ♣   continue to 4♥ or beyond.

2)   ♠ K Q J 10 5   One or two well-placed queens from
        ♥ A K 10   partner will make this deal an easy game
        ♦ A K 8   in spades or notrump. Open 2♣.
        ♣ K 4

At times you will encounter hands of 21 or 22 points that are not suited to the strong 2♣ opening. These hands have fatal flaws (too many losers) and should be opened at the one-level. The most important concern is the quality of the intended trump suit.

♠ A K Q	This hand is worth 21 points, but some
♥ K J 9 7 4	4 ½ losers, perhaps more if partner does
♦ J 8	not have help in hearts. Open 1♥. You
♣ A K 4	will not miss game if partner cannot respond.

The Response Structure

The most difficult aspect of this convention is classifying and communicating the character of responder's hand. Often it is the opener who must decide whether to press for a slam or settle for less. He needs an adequate picture of responder's strength to make good decisions. To this end, responder's hands are placed into one of these four categories.

(A) Hands of 0 to 3 points.
(B) Hands of 4 to 6 points.
(C) Hands of 7 to 9 points.
(D) Hands of 10 or more points.

If the strong hand has a minimum 2♣ opener, 8 or 9 tricks, hands of type A, B and C will not normally produce slam. As responder classifies his strength and degree of support for opener's suit, it usually becomes opener's responsibility to place the contract, mainly because his strength range is less defined than responder's. However when responder has the strength of category D, he should assume leadership in the slam decision whenever a satisfactory strain is found.

Negative Or Waiting Responses (Type A and B Hands)

The first response begins to define your strength. An artificial 2♦ is employed for all hands less than 7 points. This bid is referred to as a negative or waiting response.

1)	*Partner*	*You*	♠ 10 7 5 4
	2 ♣	2 ♦	♥ 6 5
			♦ J 4
			♣ Q 9 8 6 5

You have just three high-card points. This is certainly a bare bones hand!

2)   *Partner*   *You*   ♠ 10 7 6
        2 ♣   2 ♦   ♥ J 9 4 2
                                    ♦ A J
                                    ♣ 10 8 7 6

You have 6 high-card points; qualifying as a waiting hand to be further defined at the next round.

Opener's Second Bids

After a 2♦ response, it is time for the opener to specify his strong suit. It should be named at the lowest level available; there is no need to jump the bid no matter how strong you are since any suit call below game is forcing.

        ♠ A K J 10 2   *You*   *Partner*
        ♥ A K Q   2 ♣   2 ♦
        ♦ A 3   2 ♠
        ♣ 9 8 5

You have the equivalent of 8 1/2 tricks, needing only about five honor points from partner for a good game try. Partner calls 2♦ after which you reveal the good spade suit.

Second Negative Responses (Type A Hands)

After 2♣ - - 2♦, partner names his strong suit. Given his great strength, it is useful for you to differentiate your really, really poor hand (type A) that is worth no more than one trick from the better ones. You do this via a second negative; by calling the cheaper of the minors at the three-level - that is clubs if that suit is available, otherwise diamonds. In the rare case where partner's suit is diamonds, neither minor is available so the negative second response becomes 3NT.

1)   *Partner*   *You*   After 2♦ your next call is 3♣. This
        2 ♣   2 ♦   is the 2nd negative, limiting your
        2 ♥   3 ♣   hand to 3 points.

2)   *Partner*   *You*   Partner suit is clubs, so his second
        2 ♣   2 ♦   bid is 3♣ to show clubs are for real.
        3 ♣   3 ♦   Your 3♦ is the 2nd negative.

3)   *Partner*   *You*   Partner's suit is diamonds which he
        2 ♣   2 ♦   can only show by bidding 3♦. The
        3 ♦   3 NT   2nd negative now becomes 3NT.

After this negative second response, opener must place the contract as responder is no longer obliged to keep the bidding open.

There is one situation where the responder may pass short of game. After a negative second response, if the opener rebids his suit below game, responder should then pass.

Partner	You	♠ 7 6 4
2 ♣	2 ♦	♥ J 4 2
2 ♠	3 ♣	♦ 9 5 4 3
3 ♠	Pass	♣ 7 5 3

After your second negative 3♣, partner rebids his spades. Now you may pass below game.

Positive Second Responses (Type B Hands)

A positive second response shows a limited range of 4 to 6 points, yet it is sufficient for game. Partner opens a strong 2♣ and your first response is 2♦; then he shows his real suit. Now you may make a positive move: raise partner if you can (partner's suit is certain to be very good, so two-card support is ok); or when unable to raise, bid a suit that is likely to produce a trick; or as the last resort call notrump.

1)	Partner	You	♠ 10 2
	2 ♣	2 ♦	♥ Q 3 2
	2 ♥	3 ♥	♦ K 6 5 4
			♣ 9 7 5 4

You have support for partner's hearts and a likely trick with the ♦K.

2)	Partner	You	♠ K 8 6
	2 ♣	2 ♦	♥ 3 2
	2 ♥	2 NT	♦ Q 10 4 2
			♣ J 8 6 5

This hand will produce one or two tricks. Moreover, It has good balance and stoppers where you need them.

Positive Responses (Type C Hands)

Respond positively with seven points or more. _This action is always game-forcing_. Bid a suit if it is at least five cards and of good quality, such as one headed by A-K, A-Q, K-Q, or K-J-10. Otherwise, holding a reasonably balanced hand answer 2 NT.

1)   *Partner*   *You*   ♠ A Q 9 7 5
        2 ♣   2 ♠   ♥ 10
        3 ♥   3 NT   ♦ Q 7 4 3
                                  ♣ 8 5 4

After your positive spade bid, partner announces his strong suit. Lacking heart support, 3NT is the best call.

2)   *Partner*   *You*   ♠ Q 9 3 2
        2 ♣   2 ♥   ♥ K Q 9 3 2
        3 ♦   3 ♠   ♦ 9 7 5
                                  ♣ 8

With positive values and 5-4 in the majors you can show both suits. This is the South hand in **Deal Number 14** (see page 97).

3)   *Partner*   *You*   ♠ Q J 3 2
        2 ♣   2 NT   ♥ A 3 2
        3 ♥   4 ♥   ♦ 9 7 5 2
                                  ♣ Q 9

Here you have no suit to bid, but with 9 high-card points, a positive bid is desirable and notrump is the logical choice. Partner has the option of continuing on to slam.

Positive Responses (Type D Hands)

Here you have 10 points or more. You are going to make a positive response to partner's 2♣ opener - the same call as you would make with a Type C hand. Because you make the same initial response with type C and type D hands, partner will know only that you have 7 points or more. He assumes you are heading for game and will bid accordingly. Knowing the partnership is heading for slam, you should retain control of further bidding, aiming for slam providing you can find a good strain.

        Partner   *You*   ♠ J 8 6
        2 ♣   2 ♥   ♥ A K 8 3 2
        2 ♠   3 ♣   ♦ 10 2
        3 ♠   4 NT   ♣ K 5 3
        5 ♥   6 ♠

As soon as partner shows his strong spades, you should realize there is slam strength and a viable spade suit. After the 2♠ call, you could jump directly to 4NT (Blackwood), but the preferred route is to temporize with a forcing 3♣, allowing time to evaluate grand slam prospects. Partner's spade rebid does not show extra values so you proceed to Blackwood.

DEAL NUMBER 14

Dealer: East
Vulnerable: None

                          NORTH
                          ♠ A K 10 8
                          ♥ 7 4
                          ♦ A K Q J 8
                          ♣ A 6

WEST   **EAST**
♠ J 7 4   ♠ 6 5
♥ J 5   ♥ A 10 8 6
♦ 10 4   ♦ 6 3 2
♣ Q 10 9 7 5 4   ♣ K J 3 2

                          SOUTH
                          ♠ Q 9 3 2
                          ♥ K Q 9 3 2
                          ♦ 9 7 5
                          ♣ 8

West	North	East	South
		Pass	Pass
Pass	2 ♣	Pass	2 ♥
Pass	3 ♦	Pass	3 ♠
Pass	6 ♠ ///		

After three passes North opens a strong 2♣. South gives a positive game-forcing response showing five good hearts. North next discloses his best suit, diamonds. To further describe his hand, South bids the four-card spade suit, pleasing partner. North has all but the heart ace. Since partner bid hearts, he has no fear of two heart losers. Expecting to win four spades, five diamonds and a club in hand and two more tricks from partner, North goes for the slam.

East makes a passive trump lead. Declarer pulls trump then drives out the heart ace, which is on-side, giving declarer 2 heart tricks to easily make the contract.

BALANCED HANDS

The two club opener is a dual-purpose tool. The previous section presented it's use for strong unbalanced hands. It is used also to describe strong balanced hands. The 2♣ opener declares the character of his hand at the second round of bidding; the balanced hand being revealed when the opener calls notrump at the second turn. Recall that a direct opening bid of 2NT promises 21 to 22 points. The 2♣ opener followed by notrump differentiates the stronger balanced hands of 23 points or more; your precise strength being defined by the level of the notrump call - 2NT, 3NT or 4NT.

Opener 1st & 2nd Bids	Strength
2♣ - - - 2NT	23 or 24 points
2♣ - - - 3NT	25 or 26 points
2♣ - - - 4NT	27 or 28 points

Following are typical examples where you show balance and strength after partner responds to your 2♣ opener.

1) ♠ K J 8   *You*   *Partner*
    ♥ A Q   2 ♣   2 ♦
    ♦ K Q 6 2   2 NT
    ♣ A K J 7

You have a balanced hand of 23 points. This hand is North in **Deal Number 15** (see page 99). Partner has a mere 3 high-card points but continues to 3NT.

2) ♠ K Q J 10   *You*   *Partner*
    ♥ A K 10   2 ♣   2 ♦
    ♦ A Q   3 NT
    ♣ K Q J 6

You have a balanced 25 high-card points as evidenced by the 3NT call.

Unaware of the type hand you have when 2♣ is opened, responder always follows the rules for the four types of hands described previously. No matter what suit responder mentions, your second bid is notrump as shown in the above examples.

DEAL NUMBER 15

Dealer: West
Vulnerable: All

	NORTH	
	♠ K J 8	
	♥ A Q	
	♦ K Q 6 2	
	♣ A K J 7	

WEST		**EAST**
♠ A 7 4		♠ 6 5 2
♥ K 8 7 6		♥ J 9 5 3 2
♦ A 9 5 3		♦ 4
♣ 6 4		♣ Q 10 3 2

	SOUTH	
	♠ Q 10 9 3	
	♥ 10 4	
	♦ J 10 8 7	
	♣ 9 8 5	

West	North	East	South
Pass	2 ♣ (1)	Pass	2 ♦ (2)
Pass	2 NT (3)	Pass	3 ♣ (4)
Pass	3 ♦ (5)	Pass	3 NT ///

(1) Two Club Convention. (2) Waiting response. (3) Balanced 23-24 points
(4) Stayman. (5) Denies a four-card major.

North opens a forcing 2♣, then further describes his hand as balanced and 23 to 24 points. Following this bid Stayman is "on" and South uses this convention to determine if there is a 4-4 spade fit. Absent a spade fit South continues to the notrump game.

North is the declarer and East leads fourth of his strongest suit, clubs, to declarer's jack. Declarer counts 11 potential tricks, but must drive out defenders' two aces to obtain them. He begins with spades, forcing west to play his ace. West switches to a heart, but too late as North has two heart stoppers to hold the fort while he drives out the diamond ace, making 10 tricks.

An initial heart lead by East would allow the defense to establish that suit before declarer could establish both diamonds and spades. Then the defenders could take three hearts and two aces, setting the contract one trick.

There are times when partner responds to your 2♣ opener by calling 2NT, thus co-opting your intended 2NT call. When this happens, your second bid becomes 3NT. This notrump call at the lowest level available tells partner that you have a balanced 23 to 24 points. He may proceed to slam if appropriate, counting on your strength as thus defined. Partner needs some 8 points to chance a slam.

♠ K Q	*You*	*Partner*
♥ A Q J 6	2 ♣	2 NT
♦ A J 2	3 NT	
♣ K Q J 3		

Your 3NT raise defines balance and 23 or 24 points. If partner has 7 points, he may pass. With 8 points, it is a toss-up and a 4NT slam invitation may be a good tactic (see Chapter 12: Slams). With 9 or more, partner should proceed to a notrump slam.

If you have more than 24 points and partner calls 2NT, you must take charge and proceed toward slam because the partnership certainly has the requirements for a small slam. Usually the preferred course of action next is to use the Gerber Convention.

♠ K Q J	*You*	*Partner*
♥ A 8 4	2 ♣	2 NT
♦ A K J 2	4 ♣	4 ♥
♣ A K 6	5 ♣	5 ♦
	6 NT	

Slam is in the cards as soon as partner gives a positive response. Your 4♣ and 5♣ calls are Gerber, asking for aces then kings.

*   *   *   *

The Two Club Convention - Winning Ways

Use the Two Club Convention:
- With an unbalanced hand anytime game is possible even though partner has less than 6 points.
- With a balanced hand and 23 points or more.

Then show the character of your hand next:
- If unbalanced, bid your strong suit.
- If balanced, bid notrump next (2NT, 3NT, or 4NT according to your strength)..

Respond to a 2♣ opener according to your high-card points:
- A) 0 to 3 points: 2♦, then a second negative.
- B) 4 to 6 points: 2♦, then a positive second call.
- C) 7 to 9 points: A good suit or 2NT.
- D) 10+ points: A good suit or 2NT, then proceed toward slam.

9
WEAK TWO OPENERS

Usually bridge conventions come with price tags because they replace natural bids that have their own intrinsic values in the overall bidding scheme. Of course we would not want to lose a natural bid that has more value than the convention that takes it's place. However weak two openers (hence forth referred to as "weak twos") enhance standard bidding measurably such that in any kind of bridge game the net gain is worth the candle. Weak twos are far past experimentation, having been around since the 1930's.

Weak twos begin with opening bids of 2♦, 2♥, and 2♠. These hands contain reputable six-card suits and 6 to 10 high-card points. At the lower end of this high-card range, most of the honors are in the long suit. These specific length and strength requirements enable partner, when he has significant honors of his own, to carry on with some confidence regarding the character of your weak hand.

When your side has the elephant's share of honors, the weak two facilitates finding a good contract. When the other side has most of the honors and you open first with a weak two, this early action interferes with opponents' bidding, complicating their task of finding a good contract. A lesser noted benefit is that the weak two opener is a good lead-directing hint to partner. If the opposition is going to use this tool against you, it's only just that your side does likewise.

Opening Requirements

The weak two describes a hand with a six-card suit of good quality. As a general rule when you open a weak two, partner expects your hand to be worth about 5 tricks, with hardly any defensive values. Hence most of your high-card strength is in the long suit.

1)   ♠ 6 5   This hand has a very nice heart suit
       ♥ K Q J 9 4 3   good for 5 tricks. It is a typical weak
       ♦ 10 9 4   two opener.
       ♣ 6 4

2)   ♠ K 9 6   The heart suit is of good quality and
       ♥ K 10 9 4 3 2   the outside king may produce a trick.
       ♦ 9 4 3   It is a reasonable weak two opener. This
       ♣ 8   is the South hand in *Deal Number 16*
                                    (see page 103).

3)   ♠ Q 8   You have six hearts and six high-card
       ♥ J 10 9 6 5 4   points. But if you opened 2♥, partner
       ♦ 5 4 2   would be very disappointed in the
       ♣ K 8   quality of your hearts. Pass.

4)   ♠ K J 9 7   This good diamond suit qualifies the
       ♥ 5 4   hand as a weak two. However if you
       ♦ K Q 10 7 6 4   open 2♦, it is unlikely that you will
       ♣ 3   discover a 4-4 or even 5-4 spade fit.
                                    Pass - perhaps partner can open.

In bridge, it is always important to stay close to the bidding rules so as not to deceive partner. Even so, there are hands that do not quite fit the rules, and you must judge what course of action is likely to produce the best result, or perhaps deceive partner the least. There are hands where you may modestly defy the weak two rules, yet remain within their spirit.

1)   ♠ A K Q J 7   You are short one spade but otherwise
       ♥ 6 4 3   with ten high-card points and five tricks,
       ♦ 8 4 2   the hand qualifies to open 2♠. Partner
       ♣ 8 5   will not be disappointed.

2)   ♠ 9   There is considerable offensive value in
       ♥ Q J 9 8 5 3 2   these seven hearts. It is too weak to open
       ♦ Q 7 6   3♥, so - being sure of five tricks on offense -
       ♣ 9 2   open 2♥.

In first or second seat, your weak two openers should always be disciplined because partner has not yet been heard from. For his actions to be well judged, he must be able to read your hand accurately.

In third seat and partner having passed, you may take whatever risk you can afford to interfere with the opponents bidding; but preempting with a poor suit in any seat invites trouble.

DEAL NUMBER 16

Dealer: South
Vulnerable: None

NORTH
♠ A 4 3
♥ Q 8 5
♦ 6 5 2
♣ Q J 5 4

WEST
♠ Q 10 7
♥ A 7 6
♦ A K J 7
♣ A K 2

EAST
♠ J 8 5 2
♥ J
♦ Q 10 8
♣ 10 9 7 6 3

SOUTH
♠ K 9 6
♥ K 10 9 4 3 2
♦ 9 4 3
♣ 8

West	North	East	South
			2 ♥
2 NT	Pass	3 NT ///	

South opens a weak 2♥. West overcalls 2NT and East boldly contracts for a notrump game.

North leads to partner's ♥K, ducked by West. West also ducks the second heart lead, but is forced to play the ♥A on the third trick. Ducking two hearts is a good tactic by West as it exhausts North's hearts. If South cannot get into the lead, declarer is safe from more heart losers. Unfortunately West can find only 7 tricks before conceding the lead to the defense. South gets in with his ♠K to run hearts and set the contract three tricks.

If South had passed rather than open 2♥, North most likely would have led his fourth club, declarer taking the trick with the dummy ♣10. Now declarer would be able to pull North's clubs, conceding one club. Declarer the would be able to take four clubs, four diamonds, and one heart to make 3NT.

In fourth seat, the weak two opener has no preemptive value since opponents' communications are already well underway. Furthermore, after three passes, there is no value at all to the preemptive opener. Reopening the bidding in fourth seat with a weak hand invites the opponents, who surely have as many or more honors as your side, to compete and quite likely win the auction. In most rubber bridge formats, it is better to pass out the hand than stretch for a part-score result.

♠ 9 7   A 2♦ opening in first seat is competitive,
♥ Q 7 5   but in fourth seat you should pass out.
♦ A Q 8 5 4 2
♣ 10 7

Responses To Weak Two Openers

The discussion of responses begins with the proposition that you have complete confidence in partner's openers; you can count on his weak two's to match standard specifications and be able to confidently make a good estimate of the partnership potential. Most often the choice is between passing or raising partner's suit. But occasionally you have an equal or better suit of your own, or perhaps a hand that makes a notrump game try reasonable. A raise to any level is to play; the partner who opened the weak two is not expected to bid again under any circumstance - unless he belatedly discovers an uncounted ace or two in his hand!

Constructive Raises

Sometimes you have just enough strength and support to have a good chance at game. Partner opens 2♥ and you hold:

Partner	RHO	You	♠ 4
2 ♥	2 ♠	4 ♥	♥ K 8 7
			♦ A K 5 4
			♣ A Q 9 3

It is a fair supposition that you can take 6 heart tricks, 3 others and perhaps the ♣Q. This may not deter the opposition from a spade game, but with your quick tricks, a penalty double then would be appropriate.

Preemptive Raises

Weak two openers are preemptive, and at times you may be able to extend this impediment with little risk. Suppose for instance, at none vulnerable, partner opens 2♥, RHO doubles, and you find yourself with these rags:

Partner	RHO	You		
2 ♥	Dbl	4 ♥	♠	
			♥	10 9 5 4 3
			♦	9 8 4
			♣	8 7 6 3 2

Partner announces weakness and you have no honors. The opponents must have 32 high-card points, perhaps more - likely a slam in spades that will cost you some 900 points. Of course you should not let them bulldoze you without a whimper - jump to 4♥! Sure, you could be set two or three doubled - a good sacrifice of 300 or 500 points.

Holding a feeble hand as partner opens preemptively, your first thought should be toward the merit of upping the ante, that is raising as high as you can afford to go. If it appears the opponents will make game and rubber, you can overbid two or even three tricks, depending on vulnerability. If partner's weak opener can be relied upon to produce five tricks, add to that to the tricks your hand can supply plus the number you can afford to be set, then jump to that level.

Bidding Your Own Suit

If you have not yet passed, a basic rule is that a new suit following partner's weak two is forcing one round. Consequently, do not introduce a new suit unless you think it is better than partner's.

Partner	RHO	You		
2 ♦	Pass	2 ♠	♠	A K J 9 8 6
			♥	3
			♦	6 4
			♣	A Q J 9

Your spades are great, probably better, than partner's diamonds, and a spade contract needs one trick less for game. Bid 2♠, forcing.

Two Notrump Responses

A 2NT response to a weak two is conventional and forcing one round. It is an invitation to game and aims to find out if partner has more than a minimum and perhaps a potential side trick. This 2NT response is commonly referred to as asking for a feature. When you are uncertain about the viability of game (or slam), the 2NT response is the best way to garner more information.

Partner	RHO	You	♠ 8 7 5
2 ♥	Pass	2 NT	♥ A 10 4
			♦ A K Q
			♣ 9 6 5 4

This is an exemplary hand, further enhanced when partner opens hearts. Nine tricks (six hearts and three diamonds) look certain. If partner has an outside trick, game in hearts is well worth the try. Bid 2NT, asking for a feature.

Rebids By Opener

With the weak two opener, you have told most of your story. Pass any raise. However partner may mention a new suit, hoping you support it. Holding Q-x or x-x-x is sufficient to raise; without support, rebid your suit. Partner's other election is to bid 2NT, asking for a feature.

1)	LHO	Partner	RHO	You	♠ J 6
			Pass	2 ♦	♥ 8 6 5
	Pass	2 ♥	Pass	3 ♥	♦ A Q J 8 7 6
					♣ 10 6

Hearing 2♦, partner introduces hearts. Holding three, a raise is appropriate. The partnership has nine hearts.

2)	LHO	Partner	RHO	You	♠ J 10 2
				2 ♦	♥ 9
	Pass	2 ♥	Pass	3 ♦	♦ A Q J 8 7 6
					♣ 8 4 3

This hand does not help partner at all. Rebid your six-card diamond suit.

When partner bids 2NT looking for more information about your hand, you should answer as follows: rebid your suit with a minimum (6 to 8 high-card points); with a maximum (9 or 10 high-card points) show an outside ace or king or bid 3NT to show a solid suit such as A-K-Q-x-x-x.

1)	LHO	Partner	RHO	You	♠ A 7 3
				2 ♥	♥ Q J 10 9 5 3
	Pass	2 NT	Pass	3 ♠	♦ 8
					♣ 10 9 8

You have an outside ace for extra value. When partner asks for a feature, respond 3♠ to show this ace. Your hand is South in *Deal Number 17* (see page 107). This is an exotic slam deal (aren't they all?).

DEAL NUMBER 17

Dealer: East
Vulnerable: North/South

NORTH
♠ K 6
♥ A K 8 6 2
♦ A Q 3
♣ A Q 7

WEST
♠ Q J 8 2
♥ 7
♦ K J 6
♣ K 6 5 4 2

EAST
♠ 10 9 5 4
♥ 4
♦ 10 9 7 5 4 2
♣ J 3

SOUTH
♠ A 7 3
♥ Q J 10 9 5 3
♦ 8
♣ 10 9 8

West	North	East	South
		Pass	2 ♥
Pass	2 NT	Pass	3 ♠
Pass	6 ♥ ///		

With a hand that should produce 5 tricks, South opens a 2♥. North has 22 high-card points and realizes South must have a high honor out-side of hearts. To find it, North bids 2NT, asking South to show a feature. South's 3♠ shows the ace since North already holds the king. Expecting to be able ruff a spade, North counts 11 tricks, needing only one of two finesses to make a slam. Holding three aces, he jumps to 6♥.

Reluctant to lead away from his kings, West leads the ♠Q. South is sure of 6 hearts, 2 spades and a ruff, and an ace in each minor, for 11 tricks. One minor suit finesse must succeed. After drawing trump, he tries the club finesse and the queen holds. With nothing to lose, South returns to his hand and successfully finesses diamonds, taking all 13 tricks.

2)	LHO	Partner	RHO	You	♠ 9 8 5
				2 ♦	♥ 10 6 5
	Pass	2 NT	Pass	3 ♦	♦ A Q 8 7 5 4
					♣ 2

You diamond rebid indicates a minimum hand. Partner decides on the final contract.

*   *   *   *

Weak Two Openers - Winning Ways

Open 2♦, 2♥, or 2♠ when you have a good six-card suit and 6 to 10 high-card points. This is primarily a defensive action, yet may win the contract.
Responses:
  • Raise is to play; opener should not bid again.
  • Bid a new suit (presumably better than opener's suit), forcing one round.
  • Bid 2NT - conventional and forcing.
Responses to the conventional 2NT:
  • With a minimum 6 to 8 points, rebid your suit.
  • With more than a minimum:
    ✓ Bid a suit containing an ace or king.
    ✓ Bid 3NT to show a solid suit.

10
PREEMPTIVE OPENERS

Preemptive openers include every opening suit at the three-level or higher, theoretically all of the way up to seven spades. The objective is to collapse opponents' bidding space. For instance, when you open 3♠ the opponents are deprived of all of the bidding space from 1♣ to 3♥. They cannot show a normal one-level opener, a balanced notrump, a weak two, or even a strong 2♣ bid. Instead they are compelled to rely on experience, basing their bids on the odds of success or failure (meaning they are put mostly to guesses and gambles.)

Preemptive openers appear to be extensions of weak two openers, but this cannot be since preemptive openers were created first. They represent unbalanced hands containing suits of seven cards or longer. Usually the opening level correlates to suit length: a three-level opening indicates a seven-card suit; a four-level opening indicates an eight-card suit; and a five-level opening indicates a nine-card suit. Much like their weak-two cousins, preemptive openers should contain 6 to 10 high-card points, a good trump suit, and very little in the way of defensive tricks. Since the opponents most often are short in your long suit and strong elsewhere, your hand is nearly worthless on defense.

If, as occasionally happens, your preempt is doubled for penalties, you may be set one, two or three tricks on those occasions when partner has no help. Those occasions should not deter you provided your suit is of good quality and you are conservative at unfavorable vulnerability (you are vulnerable, the opponents are not). Keep in mind that the weaker you find partner's hand, the more likely the opponents have game or slam. This is the underlying basis for the success of preemptive bids.

Certainly some bridge players open preemptively with poorer hands. Often they succeed because doubles are usually for takeout and the opposition is unable to find good penalty doubles. There is a downside to this practice, however. Oft times partner has a hand of such good quality that the deal belongs to you. In these situations, if your preempts are not of consistent character, partner will be unable to place contracts accurately and your results will suffer, as may partnership confidence.

Preemptive openers are most effective when you are the dealer and first to bid. If RHO deals and opens, the value of the preempt declines because LHO already has a fairly reasonable notion of their combined assets. A conservative preempt still has considerable value: it collapses opponents' bidding space; it is a hint to partner regarding an opening lead; and partner may have some positive values with which to compete for the contract. On the other hand, a rash preempt in a poor quality suit can be expensive after an opponent opens as now the opposition has a good fix on where the balance of strength lies.

Preemptive openers can be effective in any seat except fourth. In first or second seat, it is quite appropriate to preempt even though partner may have a very good hand. Preempts are sufficiently descriptive to allow partner to place the contract with reasonable accuracy. Preempts in the third seat are more marginal because RHO has already spoken, but still useful in compressing bidding space - always a worthwhile action when you can afford it. The fourth-seat preempt is of little use as both opponents have had a chance to speak.

Preempting Below Game

If your trump is secure, there is little risk of being doubled below game. Any time partner's hand cannot contribute tricks, the opponents surely have game or better. However, often partner's hand is worth a trick or two, minimizing losses and increasing odds of making your contract.

1) ♠ 3 2
    ♥ K Q J 9 6 3 2
    ♦ 5 4 3
    ♣ 6

This textbook hand has a respectable heart suit and six high-card points, all concentrated in hearts. While it is too deficient in honors to open at the one-level, it is quite sufficient to preempt.

You should take six tricks in hearts. If partner has no help whatsoever, you could go minus three. But consider the alternative: if partner has no tricks, the opponents must have upwards of 30 or more high-card points and a good fit.

2) ♠ Q J 10 9 7 5 4
    ♥ 8 7 6
    ♦ A 3
    ♣ 6

The quality of spades is marginal, but the suit will take five tricks plus the ♦A. Open 3♠ unless vulnerability is not in in your favor.

If you are vulnerable, a hungry opponent holding the ♠A and ♠K and some other quick tricks may decide to convert partner's takeout double into a penalty, especially when they are not vulnerable. While your six tricks are good, you could get set three for an 800 point loss. Sometimes it is better to let the opponents have their way, hoping the next deal will be more favorable.

3)   ♠ 7   With no defense and a good eight-card
         ♥ 10 3   suit, you can take seven and possibly
         ♦ 7 2   eight tricks without help. Open 4♣.
        ♣ A K J 8 6 5 4 2

With no defense, this is a good preemptive bid irrespective of vulnerability. If partner has no help, opponents have game and quite possibly slam, but they may have some difficulty sorting out their potential starting at the four-level. Then to, a penalty double could backfire if your partner can contribute two tricks.

Preempting At Game Level

Below-game preempts are usually safe bets because doubles are usually for takeout, leaving you harmless after having done as much damage to opponents' bidding as possible. However preempts at four of a major or five of a minor are much more likely to stimulate penalty doubles. Hence you should be prepared for penalty doubles when you preempt at the game level. Note the vulnerability. With a good solid suit and not vulnerable, a four-level preempt should be at least a good sacrifice. The enticing feature of these preempts is that the poorer partner's hand, the more likely the adversaries have game or slam, and the less likely they are to find their best contract. However be mindful that aggressive opponents are most likely to double for penalty.

1)   ♠ A Q J 10 7 6 4 2   It should be a joy to sort this hand and
     ♥ 5   find so many spades - seven tricks yet
     ♦ 10 8 7   only 7 high-card points. Open 4♠ any
     ♣ 6   time the vulnerability is not entirely
                            unfavorable, otherwise 3♠.

Expect a penalty double. If partner has next to nothing and you are not vulnerable, you could go down two or three tricks for a 300 to 500 point loss - a fair price to pay to shut out the opposition.

2)   ♠ 9 8   Ordinarily this hand is worth eight tricks
     ♥ 7 5   in a diamond contract. You are safe to
     ♦ A K Q 9 8 5 4 3   open 4♦ vulnerable, or 5♦ not vulnerable.
     ♣ 3

Sometimes opponents double for penalty on principle, when they have good values but are unable to find a suitable contract. They are most likely to double 5♦, hoping to salvage something from the deal. Supposing partner has one trick to add to your eight, you would be set two tricks at a cost of 300 not vulnerable. The opponents will not be happy about this having been preempted out of a probable slam.

Responses To Preemptive Openers

When partner opens preemptively at the three-level, count on his hand for six tricks, and perhaps seven if he has a maximum. You have heard his story and there is little further information you can extract. Partner is not expected to bid again unless you call a new suit below game or bid beyond game, either action indicating an interest in slam.

In responding to partner's preempt, the first task is to determine the best strain, usually partner's suit of course. Next estimate how many tricks you hope to take (your tricks added to partner's six or seven). Now determine how high to bid - how many you can make and how many are you willing to go down giving due consideration to the vulnerability of both parties. When partner preempts at game level the process is the same in principle, but the most common action is to pass.

Raises

Partner opens preemptively at the three-level. Any action you take commits the partnership to game. You do not need many hearts to support his seven-card suit, two or three spots will do nicely. Strong or weak, when you have support and favorable vulnerability, a major suit raise to game should be nearly automatic, unless of course you are thinking of slam. The same action may apply with 4 points or 12 points.

1)   *Partner*   *You*   ♠ 9 4 2
        3 ♥   4 ♥   ♥ K 9 4
                                      ♦ Q 5 4
                                      ♣ A K 7 2

Partner opens 3♥. Should you raise? Yes, your ♥K may solidify the heart suit for seven tricks, and clubs produce two more. Also partner may have a little more than a minimum, or the ♦Q may win the 10th trick. This is the South hand in *Deal Number 18* (see page 113).

2)   *Partner*   *RHO*   *You*   ♠ 6
        3 ♥   Dbl   4 ♥   ♥ 9 5 4 3
                                                      ♦ 8 4 3
                                                      ♣ A 7 6 3 2

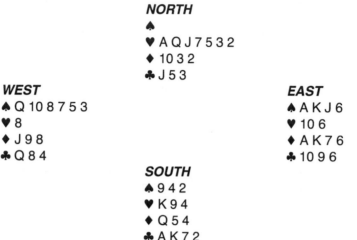

DEAL NUMBER 18

Dealer: North
Vulnerable: All

NORTH
♠
♥ A Q J 7 5 3 2
♦ 10 3 2
♣ J 5 3

WEST
♠ Q 10 8 7 5 3
♥ 8
♦ J 9 8
♣ Q 8 4

EAST
♠ A K J 6
♥ 10 6
♦ A K 7 6
♣ 10 9 6

SOUTH
♠ 9 4 2
♥ K 9 4
♦ Q 5 4
♣ A K 7 2

West	North	East	South
	3 ♥	Pass	4 ♥ ///

Holding a seven-card suit and 8 high-card points, North has a typical preemptive opener. East has a very good hand but is reluctant to enter the auction at this level. With three good hearts and 12 high-card points, South considers game potential. Hearts are likely to produce seven tricks and clubs two tricks. Perhaps the ♦Q or the fourth club will yield the tenth trick. North/South are behind in the contest so South decides to gamble on game.

North is declarer and East leads the ♠K, ruffed by North. Declarer sees nine quick tricks. He decides to try for a fourth club, and if that fails he hopes somehow luck will deliver the ♦Q. He draws trump with the ace and king, carefully preserving dummy's ♥9 for an entry. Next he plays the ace and king of clubs. The queen does not appear so he leads a third club from dummy to his jack. West wins with the queen and South's fourth club is good. West leads a spade (best play), North ruffing. Next Declarer leads a low heart to dummy's ♥9, then wins his tenth trick with the 13th club.

The opponents have some 28 points, perhaps more. Not vulnerable, raise to 4♥. RHO has barely begun to describe his hand and his partner must now enter the bidding at 4♠ or higher.

New Suits

You may have a respectable suit of your own, but unless it is a major and partner's preemptive is a minor, it is highly unlikely that yours will make a better trump. If you bid a new suit, be prepared to play it without help from partner.

Partner	*You*	♠ A K Q 10 6 5 4
3 ♦	3 ♠	♥ 8
		♦ 6 3
		♣ Q 9 5

Your spades should be as good, probably better than partner's diamonds. In spades, you should take 9 tricks, and perhaps 10.

Notrump

When partner's long suit is a minor consider 3NT as a possibility. However unless you see nine tricks in your own hand (rare), you will need to rely on his suit for a source of tricks. Partner opens 3♦ and you hold:

Partner	*You*	♠ K 5 4
3 ♦	3 NT	♥ A 8 6 5
		♦ K 6
		♣ K 9 5 2

Odds are good that you can take seven diamonds, a heart, and a spade or club. There is minimal risk that partner does not have the diamond ace and the opponents eliminate one of your stoppers on the opening lead. Even so, the odds are good and 3NT is a better bet than 5♦.

            *   *   *   *

Preemptive Openers - Winning Ways

Why you should preempt:
- Most of the opponents good bidding practices fly out the window.
- You preempt forces opponents into gambling, or meekly passing.

When responding to partner's preempt:
- Raise to game if there is a chance of making it.
- When the opponents have game or slam values, raise as high as you can afford, assuming you will be doubled for penalty.

11
PART-SCORES

In rubber bridge, having a partial game should influence your bidding tactics, in some obvious and not so obvious ways. Having 20 points toward game is hardly better than none as you need nine tricks in notrump or ten tricks in a major to complete your game; thus you should bid as though you are starting from scratch. Alternatively, with 60 points already earned, contracts of 1NT or two of any suit produce games, so there is no need to stretch further. Any time you have 40 points or more below the line, the odds are so favorable (about 5:1) that, if you can open, *always bid enough to complete the game.*

1) | *Partner* | *You* | ♠ 7 6 5 |
    | 1 ♥ | ?? | ♥ Q 7 3 2 |
    | | | ♦ Q 8 7 |
    | | | ♣ K 7 6 4 |

You are worth a single raise in hearts. When in a part-score mode, pass if 30 points produces game, raise if you need 40 to 60 points, and stretch to 3♥ if you need 70 or 80 points for game.

2) | *Partner* | *You* | ♠ J 8 7 |
    | 1 ♦ | ?? | ♥ Q 10 6 |
    | | | ♦ Q 8 |
    | | | ♣ 10 7 6 5 3 |

Your natural inclination is to pass with this meager hand, and with less than 60 part-score, you should. However, if you have 60 or more, bid 1 NT which will produce game if you can make it. Moreover If the opposition lets you have it, it is likely that your side has enough values to take 7 tricks, or the other side is missing something.

3)   *Partner*   *You*   ♠ A K J 9 4 2
        1 ♥   1 ♠   ♥ 8
        2 ♥   ??   ♦ 9 5 3
                                     ♣ 10 4

Partner most likely has six hearts, some of which are only good as trump.
If 2♥ produces game, then pass. There is no point in competing with
partner for the contract, besides your top spades will take tricks anyway.
The time to bid your suit again when you are at game level is when you
have a long but weak suit that will not contribute tricks unless it is trump
(a suit such as Q-10-9-6-4-3-2) and little else of value.

Testing for Slam

If game were the only consideration you would always bid just what
you need and no more. Unfortunately if you practice this approach
exclusively, you will miss slams and the big payoffs. Slam bonuses are
too important, too rare, and too satisfying to ignore just because you have
a partial game. Happily it should be easier to bid slams from a partial than
from scratch - because the lower the contract needed to complete game,
the more bidding space available to explore slam.

Partner Opens One of a Suit

When partner opens at the one-level, you expect him to have 13 to
20 points. If you are shy of 12 points, slam is unlikely and you may cease
bidding whenever you reach the game requirement.

        Partner   *You*   ♠ K J 6
        1 ♥   ??   ♥ Q 9 6
                                     ♦ A 9 4 2
                                     ♣ 7 6 5

You have 10 points and a flat hand. Even with this good support for
hearts, there is no slam. With 70 part-score pass; with a lesser part-
score, raise hearts to whatever level required to make game.

With 12 points or more, continue with a descriptive bid to give
partner a chance to show extra values if he has them. You will not often
get too high since then the partnership has some 25 points or more. If
occasionally you try for slam and are off one or two tricks, all is not lost -
you still have another opportunity to finish off the game.

1)   *Partner*   *You*   ♠ K
     1 ♥   2 ♦   ♥ Q 10 3 2
     2 NT   3 ♥   ♦ K Q 10 6 3
                                    ♣ Q J 10

With 13 high-card points and very good hearts, slam remains in sight, at least until you hear from partner a second time. At any part-score, bid 2♦, a positive response; partner's next bid will resolve the slam question. If he makes a passive bid such as 2♥ or 2NT, settle for a 2♥ or 3♥ contract. This hand is South in **Deal Number 19** (see page 118).

2)   *Partner*   *You*   ♠ K Q 7 6
     1 ♥   2 ♠   ♥ Q 10 9
     2 NT   3 ♥   ♦ A Q 6 4
     4 NT   5 ♥   ♣ A 10
     6 ♥

At 60 part-score, partner opens opposite this strong hand. With 17 high-card points, you are on the cusp of slam strength. Furthermore, you have good heart support. Jump shift to show this strength then support hearts. If a slam does not materialize, you are prepared to play for nine or ten tricks while needing only eight.

Partner Opens 1 NT

The two key notrump conventions, Stayman and Jacoby Transfers, are "on" following a notrump opener even though you have a part-score, thus allowing you to find the best contract whether or not slam is in the cards. In the following examples, you have a 40 part-score so you need something more than 1NT to complete the game.

1)   *Partner*   *You*   ♠ K Q 9 7
     1 NT   2 ♣   ♥ 10
     2 ♥   2 NT   ♦ 10 9 6 5
                                    ♣ A 10 4 2

With this singleton heart, a spade contract should be better than notrump. Bid 2♣ (Stayman), to investigate a possible 4-4 spade fit. Partner does not have spades, so settle for 2NT.

2)   *Partner*   *You*   ♠ 3 2
     1 NT   2 ♦   ♥ Q J 9 7 6
     2 ♥   Pass   ♦ A 7 4 3
                                    ♣ K 7

Opposite the 1NT opener, your hand is worth a contract of 3NT or 4♥, but not slam. This hand should play as well, if not better, in hearts rather than notrump. Respond 2♦ (Jacoby Transfer) and pass to play hearts.

DEAL NUMBER 19

Dealer: West
Vulnerable: All
North/South has 80 points toward game and rubber.

NORTH
♠ Q 10 9
♥ A J 9 8 5
♦ A 8 5
♣ A 9

WEST
♠ J 8 6 3 2
♥ 6 4
♦ J 9 2
♣ 8 5 3

EAST
♠ A 7 5 4
♥ K 7
♦ 7 4
♣ K 7 6 4 2

SOUTH
♠ K
♥ Q 10 3 2
♦ K Q 10 6 3
♣ Q J 10

West	North	East	South
Pass	1 ♥	Pass	2 ♦
Pass	2 NT	Pass	3 ♥ ///

North/South has a 90 part-score, needing only 10 more to complete a game and win the rubber. North opens hearts, for which South has excellent support. If North had 17 points or more, slam would be a Very good prospect. Thus South is compelled to bid 2♦ to hear another bid his partner. However North's 2NT promises little more than a minimum opener so South settles for 3♥, 2 tricks more than needed for game.

East leads his fourth club and dummy's 10 holds the trick. Declarer's only losers appear to be the ♠A and possibly the ♥K. While the ♥K is off-side, the diamonds split 3-2 so declarer can run the suit. Making 11 tricks, game and rubber.

Partner Opens a Strong Two Club

In the rare but pleasant times when you are dealt a big hand, big enough to use the Two Club Convention, do not let a part-score status deflect you from this strong opening. These are hands which have great promise for slam so it is just as well to ignore the part-score and bid the hand for what it is worth. After the opening partner shows his strong suit, responder is obligated to bid just one more time.

Part-Scores in Competition

More often than not, you are trying to complete a game with just enough values to make eight or nine tricks. Unfortunately these are the times when the opposition has some modest values also, usually enough to try to push you just beyond your comfort level. Most opponents abhor the idea of you making a game out of two part-score contracts, and they will quite often go out on a limb to prevent your doing so. These are the most competitive situations, and you should not be shy about doubling whenever they push too far. Here is a typical situation where you have a 60-point partial and a good fit, but the opponents will not let you have the contract below four:

LHO	Partner	RHO	You	♠ 7 5
		Pass	1 ♥	♥ A K J 7 2
Pass	2 ♥	2 ♠	3 ♥	♦ A 4 2
3 ♠	Pass	Pass	??	♣ Q J 8

What to do next - a most difficult question? Both opponents passed initially so clearly they are being obstructive. With your good opener and partner's minimum raise, you have a good shot at making nine tricks (five hearts, one diamond and one club, and two minor-suit tricks from partner) but not ten. Consequently you are faced with conceding the contract or doubling for penalty. What makes this choice so difficult is that a double puts the opposition into a game contract (and rubber if vulnerable). On the other hand, it is hard to see where they can get more than seven tricks, eight at the most. If you have a strong partnership, double; otherwise pass.

Opponents Have a Part-score

We turn the table and now encounter the situations where the opponents have the part-score. If you are going to stretch you bids a bit, this is the time to do it. There is a broad consensus that you may compete with an overcall somewhat light when not vulnerable and the opponents have a part-score. The purpose is to confuse them and get them to bid one too many. When you are not vulnerable, the other side has a difficult problem deciding between a penalty double and a game try; and most of the time they opt for the game try. Getting into the bidding early is a much better tactic than attempting to re-open the bidding for your side after both opponents have had a chance to bid; in which cases you invite serious penalty doubles. Here are two examples where the opponents have a 60 part-score and are attempting to complete the game.

1) | RHO | You | ♠ A J 4 |
    |-----|-----|---------|
    | 1 ♦ | 1 ♥ | ♥ K Q J 8 7 |
    | | | ♦ 8 6 5 |
    | | | ♣ 10 9 |

Your heart suit is quite good so you should not get into much trouble overcalling a little light.

2) | LHO | Partner | RHO | You | ♠ 5 2 |
    |-----|---------|-----|-----|-------|
    | | | 1 ♥ | 2 ♣ | ♥ 10 8 7 2 |
    | 2 ♥ | 3 ♣ | 3 ♥ | Dbl | ♦ K 4 |
    | | | | | ♣ A Q J 10 7 |

This overcall is light but safe behind RHO. LHO gives a minimal heart raise. Partner shows some fair values and club support with his raise, thus pushing the opposition one step higher than they need for game. This is not a sure set, but with about half of the honors, a penalty double can produce good results for your side with very little at risk.

Part-Score Amnesia

Some part-score bidding problems stem from forgetfulness, or because one partner fears that the other has forgotten the part-score. Either event can raise havoc with a particular deal. Bridge players who play both duplicate and rubber bridge are particularly susceptible to these problems because when playing duplicate they are not concerned about part-scores. Suppose you have a 40 part-score and the bidding is:

♠ A 10 9 7	You	Partner
♥ 10 4	1 ♦	1 ♠
♦ K Q 8 6 5	2 ♠	4 ♠
♣ A 10		

> You have an opening hand, and after opening 1♦, you raise partner to 2♠, sufficient for game. Forgetting the 40 part-score, partner jumps to "game" at 4♠. This jump does not feel like a slam try because it appears as though partner has forgotten the partial. But can you be sure? If it is not a slam try you may take only 9 tricks, missing an easy 2♠ game.

To avoid such complications, routinely review the score status before picking up each new hand.

*   *   *   *

Part-Scores - Winning Ways

While you may need only 7, 8 or 9 tricks for game, do not give up slam possibilities prematurely:
- With 13 points, keep the bidding for another round.
- With 17 or 18 points, jump-shift, enabling partner to evaluate slam potential.
- With 19+ points, ignore the part-score and go slamming.

Any time your side has the balance of power, do not allow the opposition to push you past game without paying a price:
- Bid again if your defensive strength is poor.
- Double for penalty otherwise.

12
SLAMS

Slam bidding is an extension of standard bidding beyond game. The first step is to determine if the partnership has sufficient strength to contemplate slam. The next step is to assess how many quick losers the partnership may have. There are three tools available to make this assessment. These tools are the Blackwood Convention, the Gerber Convention, and control cue-bids.

BLACKWOOD

Even though you have the required strength to bid slam, there remains a concern that the opposition may have two quick tricks to defeat your slam, or one quick trick to defeat your grand slam. The Blackwood Convention is used to find out how many aces partner has. Adding this number to yours tells you how many the opponents have, if any. If your side has three aces, continue to slam. If your side has four aces, you may use Blackwood again to inquire about kings if this information is helpful toward deciding on a grand slam.

	You	Partner
♠ A K Q 10 5	1 ♠	3 ♦
♥ 5	4 ♣	4 ♠
♦ K 8 7	4 NT	
♣ K 9 7 6		

You open 1♠ and partner responds by jumping to 3♦. His strength is sufficient for slam, but you do not yet know where to play it. Bid 4♣ to find out more. Partner's 4♠ settles the strain, but you need two aces in partner's hand to bid the slam. This is where Blackwood comes in. Bid 4NT asking how many aces he has. If he has but one, sign off at 5♠. If he has two, continue on.

Asking For Aces

After a trump suit has been agreed upon, 4NT begins the Blackwood process. Responder tells how many aces he has by bidding one of the following.

Aces	Response
0 or 4	5 ♣
1	5 ♦
2	5 ♥
3	5 ♠

Yes, 5♣ can mean no aces or four aces, but it is easy to determine which is correct when you consider your own aces plus partner's strength.

Here is a straight forward bidding sequence using Blackwood to assure the partnership has at least three aces.

Partner	You	
2 ♣	2 NT	♠ K 10 5 2
3 ♠	4 NT	♥ 10
5 ♥	6 ♠	♦ Q 8 6 4 2
		♣ A 4 3

Partner opens a conventional 2♣ and your 2NT is positive (7 points or more). Partner identifies his preferred suit, spades, greatly enhancing the value of your hand. Your 4NT asks for aces and partner's 5♥ indicates two. With but one ace missing, bid the slam.

Do not undertake Blackwood when the answer will prevent you from returning to your trump suit at the five-level when you are short two aces. This is not a frequent occurrence, but the possibility exists and it can be embarrassing to force yourself into an unwanted slam contract - but then perhaps you will luck out and make it any way.

Partner	You	
1 ♣	1 ♠	♠ K Q 5 4
3 ♣	??	♥ 10
		♦ K Q 6 2
		♣ K 7 6 5

Partner opens 1♣ and your first response is 1♠. Partner then jumps to 3♣ and you are on the way to slam. To avoid two quick losers, you hope to find partner holding three aces. The problem with Blackwood in this situation is, if partner has only two aces, he must respond 5♥ and you are unable to return to 5♣. Instead of Blackwood, either forego the slam or chance it directly, hoping to find a way to discard a heart loser before the opponents find two ace tricks - poor odds for sure.

Missing two aces, close out the auction by returning to five of the agreed trump suit. However there are occasions when the preferred strain is notrump, so you need a way to stop at 5NT when missing two aces. After partner has answered for aces, bid a suit that has not been bid - It must be clear that you have no interest in declaring that suit. This unusual call is a request for partner close out at 5NT.

Partner	You	
		♠ A K 7 6
1 ♣	1 ♠	♥ Q 10 3
2 ♦	4 NT	♦ K J
5 ♦	5 ♥	♣ K 10 7 2
5 NT	Pass	

Partner's 2♦ is a reverse, so you have the strength for slam. Unless he rebids clubs, this looks like a notrump contract. Commence Blackwood to be sure of three aces. No luck, partner shows only one ace. Hearts have never been mentioned so it should be clear that 5♥ is a request to terminate the bidding at 5NT.

Asking For Kings

If there is hope for a grand slam, depending on the number of kings the partnership possesses, after checking aces and finding that all four belong to your side, next bid 5NT. This 5NT is a continuation of Blackwood and asks for kings. Responses are:

Kings	Responses
0 or 4	6 ♣
1	6 ♦
2	6 ♥
3	6 ♠

These of course are the same as for aces but at one level higher. Do not ask for kings unless you wish to try for a grand slam when the partnership has the required number of kings. Also be careful that the response to 5NT does not take you beyond your trump suit when you decide to stop at six.

When 4 NT Is Not Blackwood

It should not surprise you that a 4NT call is not always Blackwood. The other use of 4NT is the quantitative notrump bid. A 4NT bid following partner's 1NT, 2NT, or 3NT is quantitative (see Slam Invitations later in this chapter).

Requirements

Blackwood is befitting only when certain conditions are present. You should know from the bidding that you have the required strength, 32 points; have a suitable place to land the contract; and be prepared to bid the slam when there is but one ace missing. Furthermore, your hand should not contain a void because then you could find partner holding the wrong ace.

Conventional wisdom advises not to use Blackwood holding a worthless doubleton. The difficulty here is that when you invoke Blackwood and discover that the partnership is short one ace, the missing ace may be in your vulnerable suit. This has been the lore for a half century, but it does not stand tall under close scrutiny.

	You	Partner
♠ 8 2	1 ♥	2 ♠
♥ A K J 9 8 4	3 ♥	4 ♥
♦ A 10 4 3	4 NT	5 ♦
♣ 8	6 ♥	

You have an excellent hand to open the bidding and partner answers with a jump shift. You can now calculate that the partnership has slam values. Your 3♥ rebid is to advise partner that you have a good six-card suit. He raises to 4♥, settling the trump question. If he has two aces, slam is a sure bet. More important, if he has only one ace, you would like it to be the spade ace because you have two quick losers in that suit. His answer to 4NT shows one ace, but what suit? Should you settle for 5♥ or 6♥? This hand is South in **Deal Number 20** where South chooses slam, risking two quick losers (see page 127).

To be sure, one deal does not prove the point, but statistics do. Finding a partnership holding some 30 or more high-card points, the odds are weighed in favor of partner having a first or second round stopper where you need it. At the slam level, odds of finding partner with the key ace or a second round stopper range from about 65% to 80% in your favor. The lower 65% occurs when partner has a minimum opener, and the higher 80% occurs when he has 17 to 19 points. In either case, the odds are sufficiently in your favor to make the wager.

What To Do With A Void

Partner initiates Blackwood and you have a void. Usually the void is as valuable as an ace, but the convention does not equate the two.

DEAL NUMBER 20

Dealer: East
Vulnerable: Both

NORTH
- ♠ K Q 6 3
- ♥ 10 6 3 2
- ♦ K 2
- ♣ A Q 5

WEST
- ♠ 9 5
- ♥ Q 5
- ♦ Q 8 7 5
- ♣ K J 9 7 3

EAST
- ♠ A J 10 7 4
- ♥ 7
- ♦ J 9 6
- ♣ 10 6 4 2

SOUTH
- ♠ 8 2
- ♥ A K J 9 8 4
- ♦ A 10 4 3
- ♣ 8

West	North	East	South
		Pass	1 ♥
Pass	2 ♠	Pass	3 ♥
Pass	4 ♥	Pass	4 NT
Pass	5 ♦	Pass	6 ♥ ///

After South opens 1♥. North values his hand at 17 points in support of spades. This strength is good for a jump shift to 2♠. South is not in a hurry, rebidding his hearts to show a six-card suit. Following North's show of heart support, South undertakes Blackwood to be sure of three aces. Finding North with the needed one ace, South opts for the slam.

To avoid leading away from his ♣K, West selects the fourth diamond. There are only three trump outstanding. If they break 2-1, there are no trump losers and declarer will have two trump left in dummy to ruff two small diamonds. This game plan works as declarer loses only the ♠A, making his slam.

There are a variety of schemes (complicated treatments) used to handle these situations. However standard bidding draws upon simple logic.

With a void, respond to partner's 4NT as usual, showing how many aces you actually have. Then if partner stops at the five-level by returning to his preferred suit and it appears that your void will supplant a missing ace, raise to six. There is some risk - but you will make these slams much more often than not.

Alternatively, if your response to partner's ace-asking bid would require you to call the intended trump suit, there arises the prospect that he will pass to play. To avoid this, jump directly to slam if you are confident of the trump suit. Rarely you may miss a grand slam but at least you will bring home the small one.

GERBER

In suit bidding, 4NT starts the Blackwood process. Where notrump is the preferred contract, 4NT is used as a quantitative invitation to slam. In these situations Blackwood is not available, so the Gerber Convention was created by John Gerber in 1938 specifically to provide an alternate way to ask for aces and kings where 4NT is not available for this purpose.

Until nearly the 21st century, notrump hand evaluations were based solely on high-card points. When a partnership had 33 points, they could be sure there was only one ace outstanding; when the partnership had 37 points, they could be sure they had all four aces. Now recognizing the value of a *qualifying* five-card suit, we have the possibility of having 33 points yet missing two aces. This new circumstance elevates the important of verifying aces along the way whenever it is feasable to do so.

Asking For Aces

In certain specific bidding sequences where notrump apparently is the preferred strain, 4♣ begins Gerber. This is the bid that asks for aces and 5♣ is the subsequent bid that asks for kings. Responses to 4♣ are:

Aces	Response
0 or 4	4 ♦
1	4 ♥
2	4 ♠
3	4 NT

The 4♦ response might seem ambiguous, but it is not. When you have one or more aces, partner's 4♦ must mean no aces. Conversely, when you have no aces, partner must have one or more. After a response, you may place the contract or ask for kings. Any bid other than 5♣ (the king-asking bid) is to play. If you wish to play in notrump below slam, bid 4NT or pass if the response is 4NT.

If the initiating partner does not want to commit to slam, he likely will close out the bidding at 4NT, perhaps in a sequence such as this:

Partner	You	
1 NT	4 ♣	♠ K J 9
4 ♠	4 NT	♥ Q 10
		♦ K Q 8 6 5
		♣ K Q 3

Your hand contains 16 high-card points and a good diamond suit, while partner promises at least 16 points. This would be a good slam try if partner has three aces. Gerber asks for aces and the response promises two. Being off two aces, close out the bidding at 4NT.

Asking For Kings

Gerber is used also to obtain a count of kings. Unlike Blackwood where you are committed to a small slam when you ask for kings, using Gerber you are able do this before undertaking the slam. The asking bid for kings is 5♣. This conventional bid can only be employed when it is preceded by the Gerber 4♣ call. Responses are similar:

Kings	Response
0	5 ♦
1	5 ♥
2	5 ♠
3	5 NT
4	6 ♣

This is the same response structure as used for aces except you show four kings by calling 6 clubs.

Here is an example where asking for kings is helpful in deciding about a small slam.

Partner	You	
2 NT	4 ♣	♠ 8 7
4 ♠	5 ♣	♥ A 6 3
5 NT	6 NT	♦ Q J 9 2
		♣ K Q 8 7

Having opened 2NT, partner has 21 or 22 points. In response to Gerber
4♣, partner shows two aces. With an ace missing, you need to account
for all of the kings. Partner shows three kings and the slam is on.

When 4♣ Is Gerber

Your partnership needs a clear understanding as to when a 4♣ bid
begins Gerber because this bid also may be used as a natural call. The
4♣ bid is Gerber when partner's last natural bid was 1NT, 2NT, or 3NT,
with but one exception: if a natural club bid had already been made, then
4♣ following partner's 3NT is natural and not Gerber. Thus, every 4♣
jump over partner's 1NT or 2NT is Gerber, and every 4♣ following
partner's 3NT is Gerber unless clubs have been previously mentioned.

1)	*Partner*	*You*	♠ K Q 6 2
	1 NT	4 ♣	♥ A Q 8
			♦ A 10 7
			♣ Q 10 7

You have 17 high-card points and a flat hand. Add partner's 16 to 18
points and you are contemplating a small slam. Your jump to 4♣
following 1NT is Gerber. This hand is North in ***Deal Number 21*** where
South proceeds to 6NT after North shows two aces (see page 131) .

2)	*Partner*	*You*	♠ K Q 8 6
	1 ♦	1 ♥	♥ K J 7 6
	2 NT	4 ♣	♦ A 3 2
			♣ 6 4

Partner's 2NT jump defines a balanced hand of 19 or 20 points. Your 4♣
bid following 2NT is Gerber.

3)	*Partner*	*You*	♠ J 10 6
	2 ♣	2 ♦	♥ 9 7 6 5
	2 NT	4 ♣	♦ A 6 3 2
			♣ K J

Partner opens a conventional 2♣ and you respond with a waiting 2♦.
Next partner bids 2NT, defining a balanced 23 to 24 points. Opposite
this, your hand is sufficient to try for the slam. Your 4♣ call is Gerber.

4)	*Partner*	*You*	♠ K Q 10
	1 ♣	2 ♦	♥ A 8 5
	3 ♣	3 NT	♦ A K J 9 7
	4 ♣	5 ♣	♣ 7 5

DEAL NUMBER 21

Dealer: East
Vulnerable: East/West

NORTH
♠ K Q 6 2
♥ A Q 8
♦ A 10 7
♣ Q 10 7

WEST
♠ 8 7
♥ 7 6
♦ K Q 6 4 3
♣ J 8 5 3

EAST
♠ 10 5 4 3
♥ J 5 4 3 2
♦ 9 8 2
♣ 2

SOUTH
♠ A J 9
♥ K 10 9
♦ J 5
♣ A K 9 6 4

West	North	East	South
		Pass	1 NT
Pass	4 ♣ (1)	Pass	4 ♠ (2)
Pass	6 NT ///		

---

(1) Gerber. (2) 2 aces

After South opens 1NT, North considers Stayman to look for a 4-4 major,
but rejects the idea because of his 4-3-3-3 distribution. North is strong
enough for a small slam, employing Gerber along the way to be certain
that the partnership has three aces.

West leads the ♦K. If the clubs behave, South can run all 13 tricks by
taking the first trick with the ♦A. However, if West has four clubs to
the jack, South will be unable to run his clubs, losing both a club and
a diamond. South doesn't need to risk the contract for an overtrick.
Almost surely West is leading from the K-Q-x-x-(x). If South ducks the
first trick, he can finesse for two diamond tricks, thus needing only three
clubs to make the small slam.

Partner insists on clubs. It should be obvious that his 4♣ call is not Gerber, having previously bid clubs, twice no less. At this point, Blackwood is still available, but with your hand there seems to be no reason to continue toward slam.

It is not necessary that responder always be the one to start the Gerber process. When responder calls notrump, opener may bid 4♣ to ask for aces.

	You	Partner
♠ 7		
♥ A K Q J 9 8 7	1 ♥	1 ♠
♦ 5	2 ♣	2 NT
♣ A K 4 3	4 ♣	

Although you intend to play in hearts, you may employ Gerber following partner's 2NT call. Partner's 2NT indicates 11 or 12 points and a semi-balanced hand. Jump to 4♣ to make sure partner has one ace before proceeding to slam. Note: even though you already bid clubs, 4♣ is Gerber because it is a jump call.

There is a rather subtle point here. Gerber applies when partner's last _natural_ bid was notrump. However responses to Stayman are not natural, hence you may invoke Stayman then bid 4♣ to start the Gerber process.

Partner	You	
1 NT	2 ♣	♠ Q J
2 ♥	4 ♣	♥ A K Q 3
		♦ J 9 5 3
		♣ Q 10 8

Here your jump bid in clubs is Gerber (even though you intend to play in hearts) because partner's last _free bid_ was 1 NT.

This same logic may apply to Jacoby Transfers, although rarely, because partner's response to a transfer request is not a free bid.

CONTROL CUE-BIDS

The control cue-bid is another tool to help assess how many quick losers you have before proceeding to a slam. Blackwood and Gerber both identify the number of aces and kings partner holds, whereas the control cue-bid tells you the specific suit wherein partner has a first or second round control. It is important to keep in mind that _the trump suit must have been established prior to a control cue-bid call_.

Partner	You	♠ Q 6 5
1 ♦	2 ♥	♥ K Q 10 9 7 2
3 ♥	4 ♦	♦ A K
4 ♠	4 NT	♣ K J
5 ♥	6 ♥	

You have a powerful hand of great potential opposite partner's opener. Needing to make a game-forcing response, the jump shift to 2♥ is a good choice. Partner raises hearts, settling the trump question. For slam you need two aces from partner. Equally important, you need a first or second round control of spades. Asking for aces will not resolve the spade concern - partner could have the heart and club aces, perhaps leaving spades unprotected. Bid 4♦. Obviously this is a slam try, and it announces a diamond control. Partner returns 4♠ - he has the needed spade control. Proceed to Blackwood to be sure partner has two aces. He does (the 5♥ bid) so you continue to slam, secure in knowing you do not have two quick losers. This is the South hand in **Deal Number 22** (see page 134).

Bidding Controls Below Game

Control cue-bids are most effective below game. Having a control (ace or king) in more than one suit, bid them "up the line", that is the lowest ranked suit first. Cue-bidding below game allows you to stop at game when the controls are not sufficient.

1)   ♠ K Q J   You   Partner
     ♥ A Q J 10 6   1 ♥   3 ♥
     ♦ 8 7   4 ♣
     ♣ A K 5

Partner gives you a jump raise. Your 21 points is just enough to become interested in slam. At this stage, a new suit shows slam interest and a control in that suit. You need a diamond control and an ace from partner. Cue-bid 4♣, hoping to hear 4♦. If partner calls diamonds, proceed to Blackwood to determine the ace situation.

2)   ♠ 6 5   You   Partner
     ♥ A 10 8 6   1 ♦   2 ♥
     ♦ A Q 9 8   3 ♥
     ♣ A Q 5

This 16-point hand plus a jump-shift equals slam, provided partner has a spade control. Partner may cue-bid 3♠, promising either the ace or king, in which case slam is on. It may seem risky to undertake slam here when partner has only the spade king as a stopper. However, if LHO has

DEAL NUMBER 22

Dealer: North
Vulnerable: Both

NORTH
♠ A K 7 3
♥ A J 5
♦ 10 7 5 3
♣ 5 4

WEST
♠ 9 4
♥ 8 6 3
♦ Q J 4
♣ A Q 7 6 2

EAST
♠ J 10 8 2
♥ 4
♦ 9 8 6 2
♣ 10 9 8 3

SOUTH
♠ Q 6 5
♥ K Q 10 9 7 2
♦ A K
♣ K J

West	North	East	South
	1 ♦	Pass	2 ♥
Pass	3 ♥	Pass	4 ♦
Pass	4 ♠	Pass	4 NT
Pass	5 ♥	Pass	6 ♥ ///

With 18 high-card points, South's slam antenna goes up when North
opens 1♦. He jumps to 2♥, game-forcing. North supports hearts, and
now South is slam-bound provided partner has a spade control. South's
4♦ is a slam invitation. North obliges with a spade cue-bid. To be sure
of three aces, South calls upon Blackwood and then opts for the slam.

West leads the ♥6. Before playing, declarer counts winners. Finding
11 sure tricks (6 hearts, 3 spades, and 2 diamonds), he looks for a source
of a 12th trick. The ♣K is a possibility if the ♣A is on side. The fourth
spade may win if spades divide 3-3. But before trying either, declarer
draws three trump then plays the two top diamonds, noting that West
plays the ♦J on the second diamond trick. This suggests that perhaps
the ♦Q may fall if he ruffs the third diamond. Now declarer has three
possible ways to win the 12th trick. He plays a spade to the ♠A, then a
third diamond, ruffed in hand. West drops the ♦Q so the ♦10 in dummy
produces the 12th trick.

the spade ace, dummy's king is safe. Alternatively, if RHO has the spade ace, LHO has no clue to your weakness and will be reluctant to lead a suit your side has bid.

3)	♠ A K	You	Partner
	♥ 10 6	1 ♦	2 ♣
	♦ K Q J 9 8 7	3 ♦	3 ♥
	♣ K 9 5	3 ♠	

Partner's 3♥ bid may a notrump try, but certainly promises a heart stopper. With your 3♠ call you have now described a good diamond suit, 17 to 18 points, and a spade control.

Bidding Controls Beyond Game Level

Control cue-bids can be shown at the five-level. In doing so you bypass Blackwood however. The cue-bid is more useful when you have a void and are not especially concerned about partner having an ace in that suit.

♠ A K Q J	You	Partner
♥A Q J 9 8	1 ♥	4 ♥
♦ 8 6 5 3	5 ♣	
♣		

With support for your hearts and 13 to 14 points, partner raises to game. Of course you are in slam territory, but the diamond suit may be a problem. Blackwood will not solve it if partner has one ace - it may be the ♣A. Cue-bid clubs, hoping partner then will cue-bid diamonds.

MAJOR-SUIT SLAMS

With modern precision bidding, much of the mystery is gone from slam bidding in the majors. Whenever partner has support for your major, you find out promptly about his support and his strength. Having done your due diligence math and finding the partnership has 32+ points, there is but one consideration before you take the dive - controls.

When partner gives you a single raise, you need 24 points in your own hand to be in slam range. In that case, you would have opened 2♣. Hence there is no chance of a slam following a one-level opener and a raise. Slam possibilities do arise when partner has a jump raise, but even then you would need a maximum 21 point opener. When partner has support for your major, you will know this and know his strength within a two-point range after his second bid, if not after the first. Often you will not know that the partnership has slam strength until the bidding has reached 4♥ or 4♠. At that point, you may check for controls.

Opener In Charge

When you open the bidding and partner has support, nearly always you are the one who must decide how far to go. This is the case when partner has between 6 and 18 points and he defines his strength and support in the first or second round of bidding. Then you, the opener, are in the better position to evaluate the total strength and decide on game if not already there, or slam.

1) ♠ A 4   *You*   *Partner*
    ♥ A K 7 4 2   1 ♥   2 ♦
    ♦ Q 8   3 ♣   4 ♥
    ♣ K 8 5 4

Partner's bidding sequence promises 15 to 16 points and you have 18 points. You now know the partnership has slam strength. The only remaining concern is the possibility of two quick losers.

2) ♠ K 9   *You*   *Partner*
    ♥ A Q 8 5 2   1 ♥   2 ♠
    ♦ 10 6   3 ♣   3 ♥
    ♣ A Q 6 2   4 ♣

Partner's jump shift promises 17 to 18 points and is game-forcing. When he shows heart support, trump is set and your 4♣ is a control bid. If partner bids 4♦, showing a control, go on to Blackwood. If not, settle for game.

3) *Partner*   *You*   ♠ A 9 7
    1 ♥   4 ♥   ♥ K 10 6 2
    4 ♠   4 NT   ♦ 7
    5 ♥   6 ♥   ♣ K 10 5 3 2

Your immediate jump to 4♥ advises partner that you have 13 or 14 points and support. Partner's 4♠ is a slam try via a control cue-bid. Now you are in position to engage Blackwood. Any two aces from partner are sufficient for a slam commitment. This is the South hand in *Deal Number 23* (see page 137).

DEAL NUMBER 23

Dealer: North
Vulnerable: None

NORTH
♠
♥ A J 7 5 4 3
♦ A K 9 3
♣ Q 9 6

WEST
♠ 10 6 5 4 3
♥ 9
♦ Q J 5 4 2
♣ A 4

EAST
♠ K Q J 8 2
♥ Q 8
♦ 10 8 6
♣ J 8 7

SOUTH
♠ A 9 7
♥ K 10 6 2
♦ 7
♣ K 10 5 3 2

West	North	East	South
	1 ♥	Pass	4 ♥
Pass	4 ♠	Pass	4 NT
Pass	5 ♥	Pass	6 ♥ ///

South's hand is worth a good 14 points and he jumps directly to game.
North re-evaluates his distribution points - 3 for the void and 2 for the sixth
trump. So his value now is 19 points, which combined with South's promised
13-14 points, is sufficient for slam. He bids 4♠ to show slam interest and
a spade control. Having first or second round control in every suit, South
Uses Blackwood to make sure there is only one ace missing.

East leads the ♠K, declarer winning with the dummy ♠A while discarding a
club in hand. When both defenders follow to the first trump, six trump tricks
Are secure. Declarer counts six trumps, one spade, two diamonds and a club.
He needs only to ruff two diamonds in dummy to make the slam.

Responder In Charge

There are those rare occasions where responder is strong enough (19+) to insist on slam even though opener has but a minimum. When you hold such a hand, it is your deal to make or break. Take your time to determine the best strain. Be sure the partnership has three aces. If you have a worthless doubleton, try to find out if partner has first or second round control of that suit.

Partner	You	
1 ♠	2 ♥	♠ K 10 8
2 ♠	3 ♣	♥ A K 8 5
3 NT	4 NT	♦ Q J
		♣ A Q 8 7

You have support for spades and slam values. There is no hurry, bid your hearts then clubs, both forcing. When partner bids 3NT, you are assured he has a diamond stopper and can safely proceed to Blackwood.

MINOR-SUIT SLAMS

Minor-suit slams are somewhat more difficult, mainly due to the natural preference for notrump. Minor-suit contracts perform especially well when the partnership has 5-4, 5-5, 6-3, or 6-4 fits, nine or ten trumps. The 4-4 and 5-3 fits often produce better results in notrump. Success depends on several factors. First is the potential of unbalanced hands (distribution values). Second, when responder bids 2♣ or 2♦ over a one-level opener, that suit should contain five cards. This rule is waived when the responder has 19 points or more. Third, a reverse bid by opener is especially useful in identifying potential minor suit slams, as they convey considerable data about openers distribution and strength.

Unbalanced Hands

Many slams are missed because of under-rating distributional hands, particularly trump length beyond an eight-card fit. You need to continually re-evaluate the hand throughout the bidding.

	North	South
♠ 9	1 ♣	1 ♠
♥ A K 9 3	1 NT	3 ♣
♦ 9 4 3	3 ♥	4 ♦
♣ A Q 7 4 2	4 NT	5 ♦
	6 ♣	

North opens 1♣, and South responds 1♠ next jumping to 3♦ (13 - 14 points and at least 4 clubs). Adding 2 points for the fifth club, North's hand re-evaluates to a very good 17 points, with weakness only in diamonds. So North cue-bids 3♥ and partner conveniently cue-bids diamonds. The final step toward slam is Blackwood to be sure partner has an ace. This the North hand in *Deal Number 24,* a 50/50 slam deal (see page 140).

Responses At The Two-Level

Responding in a minor suit at the two-level is indicative of a five-card suit unless the hand is exceptionally strong. It also requires 10 points or more giving opener a first clue to the overall partnership strength. This enables him to recognize a good minor suit fit early in the bidding.

	You	Partner
♠ A K J 4 3	1 ♠	2 ♦
♥ A K Q	3 ♥	4 ♦
♦ K 10 9	??	
♣ 8 7		

Partner's 2♦ response is indicative of a five-card suit and 10+ points. You can see that there is slam strength, but you are at risk in clubs. It is not particularly useful to cue-bid in a suit you have already called, and partner might misunderstand the bid to be a rejection of his diamonds. On the other hand, having a maximum of seven high-card points in diamonds, partner most certainly has a good honor in clubs. This looks like a good 6♦ slam.

Reversing To Slam

Often the more difficult slams are those where each hand is about equal in strength. With an suitable hand responder can often jump shift to describe a 17 or 18 point hand. But most often it is up to the opener to describe his 16 or 17 point hand, leaving it to responder to pursue the slam. These are intermediate hands that are not quite strong enough to

DEAL NUMBER 24

Dealer: West
Vulnerable: North/South

NORTH
♠ 9
♥ A K 9 3
♦ 9 4 3
♣ A Q 7 4 2

WEST
♠ Q 10 6 3 2
♥ 5 2
♦ Q J 7 5
♣ K 9

EAST
♠ A 8 5
♥ 10 8 7 6 4
♦ K 10 8 2
♣ 8

SOUTH
♠ K J 7 4
♥ Q J
♦ A 6
♣ J 10 6 5 3

West	North	East	South
Pass	1 ♣	Pass	1 ♠
Pass	1 NT	Pass	3 ♣
Pass	3 ♥	Pass	4 ♦
Pass	4 NT (1)	Pass	5 ♦ (2)
Pass	6 ♣ ///		

(1) Blackwood. (2) One ace.

South first responds 1♠ then jump raises to 3♣, forcing. This encourages
North to consider slam. Concerned about diamonds, North cue-bids hearts,
And then South's 4♦ shows the needed control. North commits to slam
via Blackwood.

Knowing South holds the ♦A, East leads his fourth diamond, hoping
declarer has only one stopper, declarer having no choice but to win this trick.
He can see 12 tricks if he can capture the missing trump king and discard
dummy's losing diamond before the defense leads diamonds again. With
three trumps out, he leads dummy's ♣J, leaving it ride when West plays low.
The ♣J holds and declarer draws the remaining king. Now he takes dummy's
high hearts, returns to hand via a trump and discards the losing a diamond
and a spade on his good hearts. Conceding a spade trick, he then fulfills
the contract by cross-ruffing diamonds and spades.

jump shift. (Recall that the jump shift requirement for responder is less than that for an opener.) A most useful way for the opener to describe these intermediate hands containing a five-card minor is to employ the reverse at the second round of bidding. This reverse is an essential tool for finding good minor slams where both partners have roughly one-half of the points needed.

♠ 9 3	*You*	*Partner*
♥ A 10 8 7	1 ♦	1 ♠
♦ A Q J 4 3	2 ♥	
♣ K Q		

You have 16 high-card points, short spades and a sound five-card diamond suit. This is an ideal hand to reverse following partner's 1♠ because it strongly implies a 5-4 profile. If there is a diamond fit and slam potential, partner should be able to recognize it.

Minors After Notrump Openers

When partner opens 1NT, you are half-way to slam, perhaps a little more. In a minor, you need 16 points and preferably a six-card suit. If your minor length is only five, the odds are _overwhelming_ that notrump will produce equal or better results. With 16 points and a good six-card minor, jump to 3♣ or 3♦ This bid expresses slam interest. (Alternatively when you wish to play in a minor suit game, jump directly to 5♣ or 5♦.)

Partner	*You*	
1 NT	3 ♦	♠ K Q 7
		♥ 5
		♦ A K J 8 6 4
		♣ Q 9 8

Your hand has 15 high-card points and a singleton heart. You can count on partner having two diamonds, assuring a 6-2 or better fit. The 3♦ jump shows slam interest.

An alternate route to a minor slam following 1NT is to jump directly to 4♣ (Gerber). Your suit must be nearly self-sustaining because partner has no idea where you are going and has no opportunity to support or deny interest in your suit.

Partner	*You*	
1 NT	4 ♣	♠ K 7 3
		♥ K Q 7
		♦ 9
		♣ A K Q 9 8 7

This hand easily qualifies for slam. However, it is not suitable for Blackwood, because partner may respond 5♦, showing one ace when you need two, leaving you unable to return to a 5♣ contract. This jump to 4♣ enables you to check for aces without bidding too high.

There are infrequent times when cue-bidding controls is a good way to investigate slam following a notrump opener, particularly when you have a worthless doubleton.

Partner	You	
1 NT	3 ♦	♠ A Q J
3 ♥	3 ♠	♥ 8 6
		♦ A K Q 7 5 2
		♣ 6 2

You have slam values but two weak suits, both without stoppers. After your jump to 3♦, partner's heart cue-bid takes care of that suit. Now you can show spade controls.

NOTRUMP SLAMS

After a notrump opener, there are several methods to evaluate slam prospects. First, size up the partnership's combined strength. Opener has already defined his hand within three points on a 1NT opener, or two points on a stronger notrump opener. With the combined strength approaching a slam, responder may offer an invitation, hoping to find partner with that little extra needed. As full slam values become apparent, it is good practice to routinely substantiate the presence of controls.

Slam Via Gerber

In most situations, Gerber is the method of choice for checking controls along the way when the strain is likely to be notrump. Usually responder is the one to recognize the slam potential and employ Gerber.

Partner	You	
1 ♦	1 ♥	♠ A Q J
1 NT	4 ♣	♥ Q 7 4 2
4 ♥	6 NT	♦ A K
		♣ A 10 3 2

Partner opens while you sort out this large handful of honors. As partner rebids 1NT, it is clear that notrump is the place to play. On the way to slam, launch Gerber. One ace is all you need and partner has it. This hand is South in **Deal Number 25** (see page 143).

DEAL NUMBER 25

Dealer: North
Vulnerable: Both

NORTH
♠ K 8 2
♥ A K 10
♦ Q J 10 9
♣ Q 9 6

WEST
♠ 4 3
♥ J 9 8 5
♦ 7 6 5 4 2
♣ 7 4

EAST
♠ 10 9 7 6 5
♥ 6 3
♦ 8 3
♣ K J 8 5

SOUTH
♠ A Q J
♥ Q 7 4 2
♦ A K
♣ A 10 3 2

West	North	East	South
	1 ♦	Pass	1 ♥
Pass	1 NT	Pass	4 ♣
Pass	4 ♥	Pass	6 NT ///

South has a huge hand of 20 high-card points opposite partner's opener. First North-South must find the best strain. In no hurry, South responds 1♥. North's second bid of 1NT completes the description - balanced with 13 to 15 points. South decides to apply Gerber, to confirm a heart stopper in North's hand.

East chooses to lead his fourth spade, an easy trick for declarer. This is a fortunate lead for the defense as a club or heart lead would give declarer his 12th trick. Declarer counts 11 quick tricks. The 12th trick must come from a heart or club finesse, or from a 3-3 split in hearts. Declarer maximizes his chances by leading toward the ♣Q after two diamond tricks to unblock that suit. This fails, losing to East's ♣K. Back in the lead with another spade trick, declarer foregoes the heart finesse in favor of trying for a 3-3 split, finding West has the fourth heart. He has one more chance, to finesse for The ♣J through East. This one works and declarer has a second club for his 12th trick.

Slam Invitations

Responder issues an invitation to a small slam in notrump by bidding 4NT following any notrump call by partner.

Partner	You	
1 NT	4 NT	♠ K Q J
		♥ 10 3 2
		♦ A Q J 6
		♣ Q 10 9

Adding your strength of 15 points to partner's 16-18 suggests a slam is in the works if partner has more than 16 points. This 4NT bid is an invitation to slam. Partner may accept the invitation by bidding 6NT, or pass to play 4NT.

The grand slam invitation is a close relative of the small slam invitation. In the same circumstances as above, when the responder jumps to 5NT instead of 4NT, the invitation is to a grand slam. Partner is expected to proceed to 7NT with more than the minimum promised, or to sign off in 6NT otherwise.

Partner	You	
1 NT	5 NT	♠ A 10
		♥ 5 4 3
		♦ A K Q 6
		♣ K Q J 6

Holding this improbable hand opposite partner's 16-18, you certainly want the small slam, and should continue to 7NT if partner has a good 17 or 18 points. Partner must take you to 6NT or 7NT, never passing 5NT.

Gerber Verses Slam Invitations

You always have the option of applying Gerber to check for aces and kings rather than using the slam invitation bids. The slam invitation does not provide assurance of three aces unless the inviter has three himself, a rarity indeed, while Gerber provides such knowledge.

The notrump slam invitation in response to a 1NT opener is useful because opener has a three-point range and the difference between a 16-point hand and an 18-point hand is significant enough to make an informed judgment about the slam.

1)	Partner	You	
	1 NT	4 NT	♠ K Q 2
			♥ A 5 4
			♦ K Q J 3
			♣ 10 4 3

You have a flat hand with 15 high-card points, and no distribution points.. If partner has 17 or 18, slam is worth the try; with 16 points, the odds are not so good. This is the type of hand where the slam invitation is preferred over Gerber.

2) | Partner | You | | ♠ A 2 |
    | 1 NT | 4 ♣ | | ♥ 7 5 4 |
    | | | | ♦ A Q 6 4 3 |
    | | | | ♣ K J 3 |

You have 16 points, including 2 points for the *qualifying* diamond suit. With at least 32 collective points, Applying Gerber to ask for aces and kings is likely to be most useful approach to slam.

3) | Partner | You | | ♠ K 5 3 |
    | 1 ♥ | 2 ♣ | | ♥ 8 5 |
    | 3 NT | 4 NT | | ♦ A 7 6 |
    | | | | ♣ A Q 5 4 2 |

Partner describes a strong 16+ points with a five-card heart suit. This looks like a notrump slam but may be a little light if partner has the minimum 16 points. Your 4NT invites to slam whenever he has more than a minimum. Note that Gerber is not available here because you have already made a natural club call.

Notrump hands stronger than 18 points are defined within a two-point strength range, so that the utility of slam invitations (asking partner to bid slam with 22 points and pass with 21 points for instance) is marginal at best. In most cases Gerber should produce better results.

Jumping Directly To Slam

There is nothing to prevent you from jumping directly to slam whenever you can account for 32 or 33 points, but it would be a bit foolish to do so without three aces in your hand. The benefit of an immediate slam jump is that it gives absolutely nothing away to the defense.

*   *   *   *

Slams - Winning Ways

BLACKWOOD: When the partnership has the values for slam and a good suit to play, use Blackwood (4NT) to be sure there are not two aces missing.

GERBER: When the partnership has the values for slam and the last bid was 1NT, 2NT, or 3NT, use Gerber (4c) to make sure there are not two aces missing.

CONTROL BIDS: When you are considering slam and are concerned about losing two quick tricks in one suit, use control cue-bids to identify first or second round controls.

MAJOR-SUITS: When one partner makes a limiting bid, the other partner must take the lead in pursuing slam:
- With a fit and up to 14 points, usually responder id the one to show his limit and the opener becomes responsible for the slam decision.
- But when responder has 19+ points, he should control the slam bidding process.

MINOR-SUITS: The best tools to find good minor suit slams are for the opener to reverse bid or jump shift at the second bid.

NOTRUMP: After opener identifies a strong balanced hand, responder may pursue slam via Gerber or the slam invitation (4NT).

13
DEFENSIVE BIDDING

Both sides compete in an auction so often that you must use every means to win good contracts, and recognize when to concede. Defensive bidd ing refers to actions your side takes to compete when an opponent is first to bid. There are always risks involved in entering the auction following an opposing opener. It may turn out that partner has nothing and the opposition has overwhelming strength, especially when you have minimal values. Holding a moderate hand, you are gambling that partner has his fair share of the outstanding honors.

There is of course another side to this coin. If you decline to compete, you will miss many part-scores and games. After all, it is as likely as not that partner has a good share of the missing honors. In each of these competitive auctions, you should continually weigh the potential loss against the potential gain. Sometimes your gain comes from a sacrifice that costs less than allowing the opposition to win the auction and make their contract.

The rules of defensive bidding are necessarily different than when the opposition is silent. New suits following partner's overcalls are competitive; do not be too anxious to bid your suit unless it is of high quality. Notrump bidding remains essentially the same; when you overcall notrump, partner knows you are strong. Two new tools, the takeout double and immediate cue-bid are available following an opponent opening; the takeout double being the most useful tool of modern defensive bidding. These competitive tools are complementary, providing you with a rich set of choices to compete for contracts. They are:

- Overcalls
- Weak Jump Overcalls
- Takeout Doubles
- Immediate Cue-Bids

Please note that the Two Club Convention is not employed here as both the takeout double and the cue-bid serve to force partner to respond.

OVERCALLS

Overcalls in the second seat carry more risk than opening bids because RHO is known to have competitive values, perhaps as good and quite possibly better than yours. If both you and RHO have minimal values, there remain about sixteen unplaced honors elsewhere. You have no idea who has them but then neither does RHO. With some good offensive tricks, enter the auction just in case partner has his share or more of these unplaced honors. Suit overcalls may be made with good quality suits and strength of 12 to 17 points. Notrump overcalls at the one-level may be made with 16 to 18 points.

You cannot overcall at the one-level when your suit ranks lower than the opener's suit; to overcall at the two-level elevates your risk, hence you should have about two points more and of course a good five-card or six-card suit. When an opponent preempts, your overcall must be at an elevated level, so to accommodate the greater risk, add two points for each level required to enter the auction - about 17 points at the three-level and 19 points at the four-level; and your suit should be a good six-card suit or a solid five-card suit (A-K-Q-J-x).

One-Level Overcalls

Four-card suits and poor five-card suits do not make good overcalls because you need a sure source of offensive tricks to compensate for the increased risk.

1)   *Opponent*   *You*   ♠ K Q 6
        1 ♣   ??   ♥ A Q J 6 5
                                      ♦ 6 5 4
                                      ♣ 9 7

Your hand has opening values and a heart suit sufficient to overcall 1♥.

2)   *Opponent*   *You*   ♠ J 10 5 4 3
        1 ♦   ??   ♥ 7 5 4
                                      ♦ K Q
                                      ♣ A K 2

With minimum honors and poor spades, this hand does not make for a good overcall.

3)   *Opponent*   *You*   ♠ Q 9 5 3
       1 ♣   ??   ♥ A K 5 4
                                   ♦ A 8 7
                                   ♣ 9 2

This hand has good defensive honors, but at best it might produce one additional trick on offense. It is more suited to a takeout double than an overcall (see takeout doubles later in this chapter).

4)   *Opponent*   *You*   ♠ K Q 9 8
       1 ♦   ??   ♥ K 9
                                   ♦ A Q 5
                                   ♣ A 10 8 5

You hand has 18 high-card points. It qualifies as a 1NT opener and also as a 1NT overcall with these diamond stoppers.

5)   *Opponent*   *You*   ♠ 8 6 4
       1 ♦   ??   ♥ A K J 10 5 2
                                   ♦ 6
                                   ♣ 8 7 6

Being a little light in high-card points is no problem here with this outstanding suit. Overcall without qualms.

Two-Level Overcalls

When you are first to bid, you can call any suit at the one-level, but you do not have that luxury when overcalling. If, for example, you have a hand you would like to open 1♦ but RHO opens 1♠ first, you are then compelled to do it at the two-level. Prudence suggests that you have a somewhat better hand.

1)   *Opponent*   *You*   ♠ 7 5 4
       1 ♠   ??   ♥ K Q 8 6 4
                                   ♦ K Q J
                                   ♣ A 6

The quality of your hearts is barely adequate for a 2♥ overcall. Nevertheless, with these well-placed honors, the overcall is worthy.

2)   *Opponent*   *You*   ♠ A Q
       1 ♦   ??   ♥ K 2
                                   ♦ J 4 3 2
                                   ♣ Q J 8 7 5

Of course you would open 1♣, but RHO is in first with a diamond. Your clubs are mediocre, the diamonds worthless on offense. This hand stands to perform better on defense unless partner has the tickets to compete. Bide your time with a pass.

3)   *Opponent*   *You*   ♠ A K Q
        1 ♦   ??   ♥ K 9
                                      ♦ Q J 10 5
                                      ♣ A Q 10 8

You hand has 21 high-card points with two stoppers in diamonds. It qualifies for a 2NT overcall.

The Gambling Notrump Overcall

An opponent opens and you have a long, solid suit but not much else. The natural inclination is to overcall, but applying some imagination can occasionally produce a small miracle.

        East   *South*   ♠ 4
        1 ♥   ??   ♥ Q J 3
                                      ♦ Q 5
                                      ♣ A K Q 10 6 3 2

Imagine you are South with this hand. What would you do after East opens 1♥? It is too good to preempt and it has seven sure club tricks. The hand is South in **Deal Number 26**, played in the 1995 Bermuda Bowl where a USA team was competing against Canada for the world title (see page 151). Joey Silver of Canada held the South hand and, after some meditation, bid 3NT! There are no stoppers in spades or diamonds; consequently a defensive lead of one of these suits could spell disaster. This deal is a classic of two experts trying to out-guess each other.

Responses To Overcalls

When you have the values to respond, you may but are not compelled to respond to partner's overcall. Often there is only a partial game at stake and you are looking for a reasonable low-level contract. The common responses are to raise, bid a new suit if you have a particularly good one, or call notrump. These are non-forcing responses. If you have game strength (opening values in your hand) and know where you wish to play the contract, bid it directly.

Raises

Any time you are able to raise partner in competition, do so without hesitation, and take the bid as high as comfort allows. Success in competition derives in no small part from depriving the opposition of as

DEAL NUMBER 26

Dealer: West
Vulnerable: East/West

NORTH
♠ K 10 5 3 2
♥ 6 4
♦ A J 10
♣ 9 5 4

WEST
♠ J 9 8 7
♥ A 8 7 2
♦ K 4 3
♣ 8 7

EAST
♠ A Q 6
♥ K 10 9 5
♦ 9 8 7 6 2
♣ J

SOUTH
♠ 4
♥ Q J 3
♦ Q 5
♣ A K Q 10 6 3 2

West	North	East	South
Pass	Pass	1 ♥	3 NT ///

After two passes, East opened 1♥. Pausing to meditate, South finally decided that, against a notrump contract, West likely would lead partner's hearts. Thus he could take one heart and seven clubs, needing only one trick from partner's hand to make 3NT. Of course a spade or diamond lead could spell disaster. South took the gamble and overcalled 3NT.

West was aware that this notrump contract was probably a gamble dependant on a long, solid minor suit. If this were the case, South most certainly would have a heart stopper. West guessed that the long suit was clubs and led a diamond. What was declarer to do? He had eight certain tricks. Diamonds would produce the ninth if the defense did not win two hearts, a diamond and two spades first. Would West lead away from a king?   Success sometimes needs luck and here South was indeed fortunate. South played low in the dummy and his ♦Q won. Declarer ran his clubs and chanced another diamond finesse, making an overtrick. A lead of the ♠J would have set the contract.

much bidding room as you reasonably can afford. If you do not show support immediately, you may find the auction has gotten too high by the time you have another chance to bid.

1)   *LHO*   *Partner*   *RHO*   *You*   ♠ A 7 3
        1 ♣   1 ♥   1 ♠   3 ♥   ♥ 10 7 5
                                                       ♦ K Q 8 7 5
                                                       ♣ 5 3

> You have 10 well-placed points in support of hearts. Your jump raise is appropriate, and crowds the opposition.

2)   *LHO*   *Partner*   *RHO*   *You*   ♠ J 9 8 4 3
        1 ♣   1 ♠   Pass   4 ♠   ♥ Q 8 7
                                                       ♦ A Q 5 3
                                                       ♣ 7

> With a 5-5 spade fit, this hand qualifies for a game raise.

Following a two-level overcall, the tactic is the same - raise to the highest level your hand can support. However, point-count ranges differ because partner's two-level overcall promises 15 points rather than 12. Hence requirements to raise are lowered by two points: raise to three with 9 or 10 points; raise to four with 11 or 12 points.

        LHO   *Partner*   *RHO*   *You*   ♠ K 10 4 2
        1 ♠   2 ♥   Pass   3 ♥   ♥ Q 7 6
                                                       ♦ 8 4
                                                       ♣ K J 5 2

> With 10 points, you may be tempted to pass and let partner play 2♥. Count on partner for 15 points, sufficient for game. If you pass and he takes 10 tricks, do not be surprised if he is displeased by your lack of fortitude.

New Suits

An opponent opens and partner overcalls - he has a good five-card suit, maybe longer, and strength ranging between 12 and 17 points. Perhaps RHO bids another suit. You have a good suit but is it better than partner's? To be better, at least it should be six in length.

LHO	Partner	RHO	You	
1♥	2♦	Pass	2♠	♠ A K J 10 6 2
				♥ 8 6 5
				♦ Q 5
				♣ 5 4

This spade suit probably is better than partner's diamonds and it is a major. If he happens to have seven diamonds, most likely he will bid them again.

Notrump

Often you have positive values but lack the support needed to raise partner's overcall, or the length to call your own suit. Provided you have one sure stopper in the opponent's suit and 6 to 10 points, bid 1NT to give partner another chance to compete. With 11 or 12 points, jump to 2NT.

1)

LHO	Partner	RHO	You	
1♦	1♥	Pass	1 NT	♠ K 5 4
				♥ 10 8
				♦ A Q 5
				♣ 10 8 7 5 4

Advise partner that you have positive values. 1NT is the only choice available and you have two diamond stoppers.

2)

LHO	Partner	RHO	You	
		1♣	Pass	♠ A 5
Pass	1 ♠	Pass	2 NT	♥ J 9 8 2
Pass	3 ♠	Pass	4 ♠	♦ A 10 9 8
				♣ K 9 2

You do not have an acceptable overcall or takeout double. Pass and wait developments. Partner overcalls a spade, raising the possibility of game. Unable to raise spades, jump to 2NT, indicating that you are a point or two short of game strength. Not sure of the best strain, partner rebids spades, leaving the final decision to you. Partner surely has six spades and seems to prefer a suit contract over notrump. You now have adequate support to bid the spade game. This is the South hand in **Deal Number 27** (see page 154).

Game Forcing Responses

At times you need to force the bidding upward but are not ready to declare game immediately. The reasons are two-fold: you may not be sure of the best contract; or you may be interested in slam. The tools available for this purpose are the cue-bid and the jump shift, both game-forcing.

DEAL NUMBER 27

Dealer: East
Vulnerable: None

NORTH
♠ K J 10 9 3 2
♥ K Q 10
♦ K 6 4
♣ 5

WEST
♠ 6 4
♥ 7 6 5
♦ Q 5 2
♣ Q 10 7 6 4

EAST
♠ Q 8 7
♥ A 4 3
♦ J 7 3
♣ A J 8 3

SOUTH
♠ A 5
♥ J 9 8 2
♦ A 10 9 8
♣ K 9 2

West	North	East	South
		1 ♣	Pass
Pass	1 ♠	Pass	2 NT
Pass	3 ♠	Pass	4 ♠ ///

East opens 1♣. His partner, West is tempted to raise clubs but, with only four high-card points, declines. North overcalls 1♠. South jumps to 2NT, promising 11 or 12 points and a club stopper. Willing to go on to game, preferably in spades, North rebids his good six-card spade suit. South accepts the spade game.

North is the declarer and East leads a low diamond 3 - 8 - Q - K, taken by declarer. Declarer begins to the ♠A and a return finesse, losing to East's ♠Q. East takes his two aces then tries a club for the setting trick if his partner has the king. No such luck. Now declarer's trump, hearts, and diamonds are all good, making the contract.

1)	LHO	Partner	RHO	You	♠ Q 5
	1 ♦	1 ♠	Pass	2 ♦	♥ A 9 8 4
					♦ A 10
					♣ K Q 9 7 2

You have game values but the best contract is not immediately clear. Perhaps partner has six good spades, or a decent secondary suit. Certainly you have a good try at 3NT if nothing else appears more attractive. This cue-bid promises at least game strength.

2)	LHO	Partner	RHO	You	♠ K 10 9 5
	1 ♦	1 ♠	Pass	3 ♣	♥ A J 9
					♦ 9 8
					♣ A K 9 2

Clearly you want to play this deal in spades, but in game or slam? Nominally, the jump shift shows 17 to 18 points, and if you bid game next (spades or notrump) that is what partner should expect. Alternatively you may rarely be strong enough to press on to slam yourself - if you can find partner with a diamond stopper.

Responses To 1NT Overcalls

The 1NT overcall requires the same strength as the 1NT opening bid. Responder's actions follow the same rules in both situations. Additionally, the notrump conventions - Stayman, Jacoby transfers, and Gerber - are "on".

W EAK JUMP OVERCALLS

At an early stage of contract bridge, jump overcalls described very strong hands. Because we now have other ways to describe strong hands, jump overcalls are made with relatively weak hands, and are referred to as "weak jump overcalls". This means that you can compete successfully with preemptive-type hands - essentially 6 to 11 high-card points and lengthy, meaty suits. These jump overcalls require essentially the same types of hands as do weak two openers and higher level preemptive openers. Do not opt for a jump overcall with a hand that is good enough to overcall.

Opponent	You	♠ A Q J 8 6 4
1 ♦	2 ♠	♥ 7 5
		♦ 8 5 4
		♣ Q 3

This hand precisely fit's the specifications for a weak jump overcall, 6 to 10 high-card points mostly concentrated in a good six-card suit.

To overcall at higher levels you should have one more trump card for each increased level just as is required to make a preemptive opening bid.

Opponent	You	♠ J 7
1 ♥	3 ♦	♥ 10 9 5
		♦ A K 10 8 7 6 2
		♣ 4

With 8 high-card points, and quite good diamonds, this is equivalent to a three-level preemptive opener, and qualifies to jump overcall.

Responses to Weak Jump Overcalls

When partner makes a weak jump overcall, most of the time you are in the fourth seat and both opponents have already spoken. There is little more you can do in a preemptive way. Bid on to a game if you are strong enough, otherwise pass and hope partner's preempt has already done its damage.

1)	LHO	Partner	RHO	You	♠ Q 4 3
	1 ♦	2 ♠	Pass	4 ♠	♥ A K 7 4
					♦ 6 4
					♣ A K 6 4

RHO has passed, so it seems that LHO has a minimum hand. Game is almost assured - you can expect to take 6 spades, 2 hearts and 2 clubs.

2)	LHO	Partner	RHO	You	♠ 7 6 5
	1 ♦	2 ♠	Pass	Pass	♥ K J 6 5
					♦ A 4
					♣ 8 6 5 3

You could compete to 3♠ but with RHO passing, this looks like a good place to rest.

3)	LHO	Partner	RHO	You	♠ Q J 3
	1 ♥	2 ♠	3 ♥	Pass	♥ 7 6
					♦ K J 5
					♣ 10 8 7 3 2

You might consider a raise but then that action might just push the opponents into a good game contract in hearts. Both opponents have bid so they already have a good fix on their potential.

TAKEOUT DOUBLES

In the beginning "double" was intended as a device to deter opponents from making rash bids, imposing substantial penalties for having done so. Because the penalty double has very little use in the opening round of bidding, "double" was given a different assignment - that is for takeout. Most commonly used following an opponent's opening bid, double by the next bidder indicates opening strength and requests partner to call one of the unbid suits. In other words the takeout double is equivalent to saying: "don't leave my double stand, partner, I didn't mean it as a penalty double. Please tell me your longest of the unbid suits."

Why do we need this takeout double? Most certainly and quite frequently we are dealt hands of opening strength that do not contain a long enough suit to overcall, or in other instances are too strong to overcall. The takeout double serves as the primary means to enter the bidding under such circumstances. Standard bidding recognizes three types of takeout doubles. These are:

- Type I: Hands with opening values or better and three-card plus length in each of the unbid suits - the classic takeout application. Strength requirements are approximately opening values or better.
- Type II: Hands containing a very good suit that are too strong to overcall. These hands value at 17 to 20 points.
- Type III: Hands with balanced distribution and stoppers in the opponent's suit that are a bit too strong for a 1NT overcall. The range for these hands is 19 to 20 points.

Type I: The Classic Takeout

RHO begins the auction. Next to bid, you have opening strength but lack a good suit to overcall. Your distribution in the unbid suits may be 5-4-4, 4-4-4 or 4-4-3. When you double and partner answers with his longest suit, you expect to play in a 4-4 fit most of the time but with luck you may find partner with a respectable five-card suit. At times you may end in 4-3 trump suit, an unexciting trump combination but still acceptable, particularly at a low-level contract. The key to successful classic takeout doubles is to *be prepared by having honors in the unbid suits and shortness in the opponent's suit*. The use of the takeout double to show opening strength irrespective of distribution is not standard.

1) | RHO | You | ♠ K J 8 |
    | 1 ♦ | Dbl | ♥ A 8 5 4 |
    | | | ♦ 6 5 |
    | | | ♣ A Q 9 2 |

You have 14 high-card points but no five-card suit. What you want most is to discover partner's longest suit, excluding diamonds of course. And so you double, which asks partner for precisely that information. It would be nice to hear partner respond 1♥, but you are prepared to hear 1♠ or 2♣. If necessary you can play a part-score contract in a 4-3 spade fit. If partner is bereft of values, the opponents are not likely to let you have the contract, so they will let you off the hook, so to speak, and relieve partner of the obligation to respond.

2) | RHO | You | ♠ 10 7 |
    | 1 ♠ | Dbl | ♥ A J 3 2 |
    | | | ♦ K J 7 |
    | | | ♣ A Q 6 3 |

RHO opens 1♠. If you double, partner must respond at the two-level, often with less than 6 points. Thus it is prudent to have a little better than minimum. Here you have 15 honor points - this strength in the unbid suits mitigates the risk of contracting for eight tricks.

On occasion, both opponents may enter the bidding before you have an opportunity to speak. Even so, with an appropriate distribution you may still employ the takeout double. Now you need length and some strength in the remaining two unbid suits.

1) | LHO | Partner | RHO | You | ♠ 6 4 3 |
    | 1 ♦ | Pass | 1 ♠ | Dbl | ♥ K Q 8 6 |
    | | | | | ♦ 8 |
    | | | | | ♣ A Q J 8 4 |

Perhaps a 2♣ bid would work out, but it is preferable to keep options open for both unbid suits. This double asks partner to bid the longer of the two. Odds are quite good that he will have support for one of them.

2) | LHO | Partner | RHO | You | ♠ A 10 4 2 |
    | | | Pass | Pass | ♥ J 9 7 5 |
    | 1 ♦ | Pass | 1 ♥ | Dbl | ♦ 7 4 |
    | 2 ♣ | 2 ♠ | | | ♣ A Q 2 |

With 11 high-card points, you are just shy of opening strength. However after two bids by the opponents, your hand looks better, so you double. Although partner may pass following LHO's 2♣ call, holding some positive values and four spades he bids 2♠, confident that your side has a 4-4 spade fit. This is **Deal Number 28** (see page 159).

DEAL NUMBER 28

Dealer: East
Vulnerable: North/South

NORTH
♠ K Q 6 5
♥ 3
♦ A 10 6 3
♣ J 9 6 3

WEST
♠ 9 7
♥ A K Q
♦ Q 9 8 5
♣ K 10 7 5

EAST
♠ J 8 3
♥ 10 8 6 4 2
♦ K J 2
♣ 8 4

SOUTH
♠ A 10 4 2
♥ J 9 7 5
♦ 7 4
♣ A Q 2

West	North	East	South
		Pass	Pass
1 ♦	Pass	1 ♥	Dbl
2 ♣	2 ♠ ///		

South, being a little short of opening strength, passes the first round. But after the opponents bid diamonds and hearts, South doubles, hoping to find partner with some values in spades or clubs. North responds to the takeout with a 2♠ bid, and there the bidding ends. With 12 points, North is perhaps good enough to jump to 3♠, but is reluctant because of South's initial pass.

East leads a low diamond, West's first-bid suit, to the ♦Q and North's ♦A. Declarer North can see only three tricks outside of spades, so he needs five trumps to make the contract. He concedes a heart trick, intending to ruff hearts in his hand. The defense continues diamonds, forcing declarer to ruff the third diamond in the dummy. He ruffs a heart, returns to dummy via the ♣A and ruffs another heart. Conceding a club trick to the ♣K, declarer now is able to win a club and three spades, for a total of eight tricks. He may be able to gain one more trick by continuing to cross-ruff hearts and diamonds.

When you double, often you will have a 4-4-3 distribution in the unbid suits. You run the risk that partner will respond in your three-card suit. This is not an infrequent occurrence, and you should expect to play part-score contracts with 4-3 fits occasionally. Prudence suggests you should have something better than three spots; a three-card suit headed by a king or better is recommended.

Although not so common, you may double for takeout after you have opened the bidding so long as it is your first opportunity.

♠ K 10 9 8	*You*	*LHO*	*Partner*	*RHO*
♥ 5	1 ♦	1 ♥	Pass	Pass
♦ A Q 10 2	Dbl			
♣ A J 9 4				

Sometimes, but not often, an opponent does you a favor. Here it would be impossible to describe this distribution without LHO's heart overcall. This double asks partner to bid the longest of the unbid suits, assuring him that you have three good suits and few if any hearts.

Naturally you want to compete when you have opening values, but there are occasions when it is not appropriate, especially when you have a minimum hand and a weakness in one of the unbid suits. It may be prudent to pass with 13 points or so rather than chance finding a fit but instead finding a poor 4-2 trump holding.

RHO	*You*	♠ Q 7
1 ♥	Pass	♥ A 7
		♦ A Q 9 5
		♣ J 9 8 7 6

You have 13 points and both minors. You cannot support spades and both minors are deficient as overcall suits, clubs being too weak and diamonds too short.

Type II: Strong Hands With A Very Good Suit

At times you may find yourself with a strong one-suited hand, but before your turn, RHO opens. You can distinguish these hands from minimum strength hands by doubling instead of overcalling. Partner expects you to have the classic takeout distribution, and will respond accordingly. However your second call clarifies your intention.

With 17 To 18 Points

LHO	Partner	RHO	You	
		1 ♥	Dbl	♠ A K Q 9 7 6
Pass	2 ♣	Pass	2 ♠	♥ 9 7
				♦ K 9
				♣ A 7 3

This hand is worth 17 points (more if partner has spade support). Double then show these super spades. In this manner you describe a hand of 17 or 18 points and a good six-card (or solid five-card) suit. Partner needs about 8 points to carry on to game.

With 19 To 20 Points

LHO	Partner	RHO	You	
		1 ♥	Dbl	♠ A K Q 9 8 5 3
Pass	2 ♣	Pass	3 ♠	♥ 5
				♦ 10 3
				♣ A J 5

Although containing only 14 high-card points, your hand with it's seven spades and short suits rates about 20 points. If partner has no more than a couple of spade spots and two well-placed honors, game will be an excellent try. Your jump to 3♠ defines this hand rather precisely. It is a temptation to jump to game, but keep in mind that partner was forced to bid and may have nothing of value.

Inasmuch as bidding your own suit after having doubled for takeout shows a strong hand and a nearly solid suit, it should never be used to describe a lesser hand.

RHO	You	
1 ♥	Pass	♠ A 9 7 6
		♥ 10 3
		♦ A Q 9 8 7
		♣ J 6

It is tempting to double, hoping partner responds in spades or diamonds, either suit serving as a safe haven. If instead partner says 2♣, you could correct to 2♦. The compelling reason not to use this procedure is that, if you do (double then correct to another suit), partner will count on you for at least 17 points. Such flagrant violation of bidding standards will most certainly erode partnership confidence, sooner rather than later.

Type III: Balanced Hands

The third application of the takeout double is to describe a balanced or nearly balanced hand of 19 or 20 points containing at least one stopper in the opponent's suit. This indirect or two-step notrump process (double followed by a notrump call) enables you to distinguish the 19- or 20-point hands from the 16- to 18-point hands which you show by overcalling 1NT.

LHO	Partner	RHO	You	♠ A 6 4
		1 ♥	Dbl	♥ K Q 7
Pass	1 ♠	Pass	1 NT	♦ A Q 9 8
				♣ K J 6

You have good heart stoppers, balance, and 19 high-card points. Double for takeout then bid notrump to complete the description. This indirect notrump call always implies more strength than a direct notrump overcall.

With a strong hand (19 or 20 points), you do not need to support all three unbid suits; support for two may be sufficient. If partner answers in one of your two suits, you have a fit. If on the other hand, he answers in your poor suit, you can correct to notrump.

LHO	Partner	RHO	You	♠ A K 8 7
		1 ♦	Dbl	♥ 8 4
Pass	1 ♥	Pass	1 NT	♦ A Q J
				♣ K Q 8 5

Here you have good support for spades and clubs in case partner responds in either of these suits. Alternatively if he calls hearts, your week suit, you are well prepared to correct to notrump - because you have the required diamond stoppers and 19 high-card points.

When you double a major, often partner responds at the two-level. When this response is in your weak suit, you must correct to 2NT. This process still shows 19 or 20 points, but of course the risk at 2NT is somewhat greater than 1NT.

A double followed by a jump in notrump shows a stronger hand, thus it should reflect 21 points or more. There are certain hands where this process is better than a 2NT overcall (21 to 22 points).

LHO	Partner	RHO	You	♠ 4
		1 ♦	Dbl	♥ A K Q 7
Pass	1 ♠	Pass	2 NT	♦ A 5
				♣ A Q J 6 5

Your hand contains 20 high-card points and a very good club suit. This would qualify for a 2NT overcall except for the singleton spade. If partner responds clubs or hearts, you have a good fit. Instead if he responds in spades, you now can safely go to notrump, jumping to show 21 points.

Suit Responses To Takeout Doubles

In response to partner's takeout, you are expected to name your longest of the unbid suits. You may not pass with less than 6 points because this action would convert a takeout into a penalty double - that is unless there is an intervening bid by RHO, in which case you may pass with a worthless hand. With 6 points or more make a positive response.

0 to 5 Points

Respond as minimally as possible, keeping in mind that notrump is a positive response. Thus with less than 6 points, you must bid a suit. Make this bid at the one-level whenever possible, perhaps forgoing a longer minor in favor of a shorter major.

LHO	Partner	RHO	You	
1♦	Dbl	Pass	1♠	♠ 8 7 3 2
				♥ 5 4
				♦ K 3
				♣ 9 8 5 3 2

You may not pass as this would convert partner's takeout into a penalty double, which of course would be foolish given your barrenness. Fortunately you have four spades, and that suit is preferable to clubs as it keeps the bidding at the one-level.

Bidding choices are not always pleasant and can at times be downright uncomfortable, especially following partner's takeout; you are obliged to respond even with no values.

LHO	Partner	RHO	You	
1♦	Dbl	Pass	1♥	♠ 9 8
				♥ 10 9 5
				♦ 6 5 3 2
				♣ 10 7 6 4

Partner insists on a call from you. The only useful decision you can make is to keep the bidding at the one-level. With no values, keep the bidding as low as you can. After all, you are the one who will become declarer so be kind to yourself.

Sometimes an opponent lets you off easy. When partner doubles and RHO enters a bid, you need not bid. With 0 to 5 points, this is a good time to pass.

LHO	Partner	RHO	You	♠ 8 7 5 4
1 ♦	Dbl	1 ♠	Pass	♥ 9 7
				♦ 5 4 3
				♣ K 9 6 5

RHO's intervening call negates partner's force, allowing you to pass, which you are pleased to do here. A bid in this situation would show positive values, more than five points.

6 To 9 Points

Holding 6 to 9 points places you in the minimally positive range. Frequently your first response to the takeout is the same as when you have less than six points - your longest suit at the lowest level available. Now, however, you can respond at the two-level more securely, and you may respond rather than pass in the event RHO intervenes.

LHO	Partner	RHO	You	♠ A 10 2
1 ♥	Dbl	Pass	2 ♦	♥ 4 3 2
				♦ 9 8 6 5 4
				♣ K 10

These five diamonds should make a satisfactory trump suit. Note that skipping over spades tells partner that you do not have four of them.

11 To 12 Points:

Holding 11 to 12 points places the partnership close to game. After partner's takeout, you should take action that suggests invitational strength, enabling partner to judge game prospects with some degree of accuracy. To identify these invitational hands following partner's takeout, jump bid in your longest suit (no less than four cards). Alternatively, jump in notrump with balance and appropriate stoppers.

LHO	Partner	RHO	You	♠ A J 8
1 ♦	Dbl	Pass	2 ♥	♥ K 9 8 2
				♦ 8 6 5
				♣ K 5 4

You have 11 high-card points, and all honors are in the unbid suits where they complement partner's hand. You do not need a five-card suit to make this jump bid.

Note that these jump bids are at the two-level, allowing adequate room for partner to show a Type II or Type III takeout without fear of bidding too high.

Competitive bidding is not always easy. Success involves judgment derived from experience, often luck, and especially good bidding technique. Suppose you are South and the bidding proceeds as follows:

West	North	East	South	
1 ♠	Dbl	2 ♠	3 ♣	♠ 6
3 ♠	4 ♣	Pass	?	♥ A J 4
				♦ Q 9 6 4
				♣ J 9 8 5 4

With shortness in the opponents' suit and values in every unbid suit, this looks like an excellent fit. If East had passed, you would jump to 3♣, so you should have no qualms about this 3♣ call. Partner likes your clubs and raises to four, indicating somewhat better than minimal values. Should you settle for the part score or go for game? This hand is South in **Deal Number 29** (see page 166). Desperately needing a game, South stretches to 5♣.

13 Plus Points

It is somewhat rare to have a 13+ hand when two prior bids indicating opening strengths have been made. Nevertheless when you do get one opposite partner's takeout double, you should be looking for game providing you can find an acceptable strain. These hands are noted by immediately cue-bidding the opponent's suit (always forcing). Do not jump directly to game as partner may not have a Type I hand.

1)	LHO	Partner	RHO	You	
	1 ♦	Dbl	Pass	2 ♦	♠ A J
					♥ K 9 8 2
					♦ J 2
					♣ K J 8 7 6

Discounting the ♦J, with five honors working in three suits, the hand is worth a good bit more than 13 points. Cue-bid 2♦, announcing your strength and buying time to discover more about partner's hand.

2)	LHO	Partner	RHO	You	
	1 ♦	Dbl	Pass	2 ♦	♠ A 7
					♥ 6 5 3
					♦ A Q 4
					♣ K 9 8 4 2

You have no immediate interest in the majors and excellent diamond stoppers. Your cue-bid is a waiting tactic - waiting to find out what type of takeout partner has.

DEAL NUMBER 29

Dealer: West
Vulnerable: None

<pre>
                              NORTH
                              ♠ A 2
                              ♥ Q 3 2
                              ♦ K J 10 5
                              ♣ K Q 10 6
        WEST   EAST
        ♠ K Q J 10 7 5 4   ♠ 9 8 3
        ♥ 8 7 6   ♥ K 10 9 5
        ♦ 7 3   ♦ A 8 2
        ♣ A   ♣ 7 3 2
                              SOUTH
                              ♠ 6
                              ♥ A J 4
                              ♦ Q 9 6 4
                              ♣ J 9 8 5 4
</pre>

West	North	East	South
1 ♠	Dbl	2 ♠	3 ♣
3 ♠	4 ♣	Pass	5 ♣ ///

North's takeout double implies shortness in spades and values in the other three suits. South, with only 8 honor points but an outstanding fit for North, would be remise not to bid his longest suit over East's ♠2. North's raise to four confirms a good club fit and somewhat better than an opening hand. This raise increases the value of South's fifth club. South is faced with the Difficult decision - to play for part score or stretch for game. If North-South have about 24 high-card points concentrated in three suits, missing one or two key honors, game odds rate to be about 50-50, for most bridge players well worth the risk.

On a spade lead, South must lose the two minor suit aces, and potentially one heart. The only chance for eleven tricks is to find East with the ♥K and Hope he must lead hearts at some point in the play. South draws trump and ruffs a second spade. Now he plays the diamonds, putting East in the lead with the ♦A. If East leads a spade, declarer will ruff and sluff a heart loser. If East leads a heart, declarer will duck to his ♥Q, then make the contract with another heart finesse. East smartly leads a diamond, setting the contract later with a heart trick.

Notrump Responses To Takeout Doubles

Any time you have some strength, a stopper or two in the opponent's suit, and reasonable balance, notrump should be the first consideration.   Notrump responses to takeout doubles are always positive, so do not bid them with less than 6 points. Additionally, keep in mind that you do not need stoppers in the unbid suits; partner has them.

1)	RHO	Partner	RHO	You	♠ K 6 5
	1♦	Dbl	1♠	1 NT	♥ 9 7
					♦ K 5 4
					♣ J 6 5 3

Having diamond and spade stoppers presents a choice of 1NT or 2♣. Notrump is preferred because it is more descriptive and it keeps the bidding at the one-level.

2)	LHO	Partner	RHO	You	♠ A 9 2
	1♦	Dbl	Pass	2 NT	♥ 6 5
					♦ K J 7 6
					♣ Q J 9 2

With a diamond stopper or two, a balanced 11 points, and no four-card major. 2NT is the best choice. There is no reason to be fearful of hearts as partner undoubtedly has values there.

In the above examples you may assume partner has a Type I takeout. If he does, his hand should be amenable to a notrump contract since your notrump response assures a stopper in the opponents' suits. Similarly if he has a Type III (strong and balanced) he will be particularly pleased to hear your notrump call; and most likely will proceed to 3NT in either case.

The primary concern here is how to respond when you have game strength - that is a hand with which you are tempted to respond to a takeout with a game bid of 3NT. Instead it is better usually to show such strength with a cue bid, thus allowing time to hear what type of takeout partner has.

	LHO	Partner	RHO	You	♠ 10 5
	1♥	Dbl	Pass	2♥	♥ A Q 5
					♦ A Q 10 7 6
					♣ Q 9 2

Here you have game strength and good heart stoppers. This immediate cue bid shows strength; is forcing; and allows partner to announce what type of takeout he has and to do so efficiently below game.

Passing For Penalties

It is a rare hand that will fare better passing partner's takeout double. You must have sure defensive tricks, lots of them, and be nearly worthless on offense. There is little point in undertaking the risk of converting a takeout into a penalty double to gain 50 or 100 points. When you do pass for penalties, expect partner to be quite on edge until you take the setting trick.

LHO	Partner	RHO	You	♠ K Q J 9 3
		1 ♠	Pass	♥ Q 5 2
Pass	Dbl	Pass	Pass	♦ 6 2
				♣ A

Just when you are prepared to open 1s, RHO gets there first. You are unable to bid after RHO opens in your best suit. When partner doubles, you could takeout into notrump, but the prospects of reaping a big gain by converting partner's double into a penalty should be irresistible.

Doubler's Second Bid

Partner responds to your takeout with his longest suit, and no further bid should be considered unless you have 17 points or unless partner jumps or cue-bids. When he makes an economical response (most typical), game is unlikely.

Type I Takeouts

Having a distribution that will accommodate any unbid suit, the trump-to-be is whatever partner chooses. Your remaining concern is how high to go. With less than 17 points, pass. With 17 to 18 points, raise and with 19 to 20 points, jump raise.

1)	LHO	Partner	RHO	You	♠ A 9 8 5
			1 ♥	Dbl	♥ 4 2
	Pass	1 ♠	Pass	Pass	♦ A Q 9 3
					♣ Q J 4

You have a spade fit but a minimum values. Pass and play for part-score if the opponents do not object.

2)

LHO	Partner	RHO	You
		1 ♥	Dbl
2 ♣	2 ♠	Pass	3 ♠

♠ A Q 6 4
♥ 9
♦ A J 7 5 4
♣ A 7 2

Partner gives a free response. With 17 points, game is possible. Raise partner's suit to show intermediate strength.

3)

LHO	Partner	RHO	You
		1 ♥	Dbl
Pass	1 ♠	Pass	3 ♠

♠ A Q 9 7
♥ 5
♦ A J 10 6 5
♣ A K 2

Here partner shows 0 to 9 points. You have a good 20-point hand yet still cannot be sure of game. Jump to 3♠ to show a fit and 19 to 20 points.

Responding to your takeout, partner sometimes has a hand good enough to jump a level to show an invitational hand. If you are a little shy of a full opening hand, pass. But with somewhat better hand, go for it.

LHO	Partner	RHO	You
		1 ♦	Dbl
Pass	2 ♥	Pass	4 ♥

♠ A Q 3
♥ K 5 3 2
♦ 10 7
♣ K Q 8 6

At your request, partner gives you his longest suit. Having jumped to 2♥, he promises 11 or 12 points. Your hand is easily good enough to continue to game.

When partner is strong enough for game, he may cue-bid. You may extend the cue-bid, thus insisting that partner selects the suit.

LHO	Partner	RHO	You
		1 ♦	Dbl
Pass	2 ♦	Pass	3 ♦

♠ A 9 7 6
♥ K J 7
♦ 9 4
♣ K Q 8 7

In response to your takeout, partner cue-bids 2♦ to indicate game values. You still need partner to pick a suit, so you extend the cue-bid, also announcing a type I takeout.

Type II Takeouts

You have an unbalanced hand that is too strong to overcall. Double for takeout then bid your suit, promising a very good suit and 17 to 18 points. A jump promises 19 to 20 points.

1)
LHO	Partner	RHO	You	♠ J 9 8
		1 ♦	Dbl	♥ A Q J 7 5 4
Pass	1 ♠	Pass	2 ♥	♦ A 6
				♣ K J

Your 2♥ declares a type II takeout with invitational (17 to 18 points) strength.

2)
LHO	Partner	RHO	You	♠ 8 7
		1 ♦	Dbl	♥ A K Q 10 6 5
Pass	1 ♠	Pass	3 ♥	♦ 9 5
				♣ A K J

Your hand is nearly strong enough for game without help. Jump to 3♥ announcing a type II hand with 19 or 20 points.

3)
LHO	Partner	RHO	You	♠ A K Q 8 7 5
		1 ♥	Dbl	♥ 4
Pass	3 ♦	Pass	4♠	♦ 9 8 2
				♣ A K 6

Partner gives you a jump response (11-12 points). The combined strength is 29 or 30 points, easily enough for the spade game.

4)
LHO	Partner	RHO	You	♠ A Q J 6 5 4
		1 ♦	Dbl	♥ K J 7
Pass	2♦	Pass	2 ♠	♦ 4
				♣ K Q 9

Partner responds with a cue bid. With 18 points, there is a distinct possibility of slam here. Bid 2♠, showing Type II.

Type III Takeouts

Type III takeouts are balanced hands of 19 to 20 points. Whatever partner's response to your takeout, a notrump call defines this hand, and it is then partner's choice where to take the bidding.

1)
LHO	Partner	RHO	You	♠ A 3 2
		1 ♥	Dbl	♥ A Q 7 3
Pass	1 ♠	Pass	1 NT	♦ A K 5 4
				♣ K 9

The correction to 1NT describes a hand too strong to overcall 1NT, a hand of 19 or 20 points. With a good six points, partner should continue to 3NT or 4♠.

2)	LHO	Partner	RHO	You	♠ A Q 8
			1 ♣	Dbl	♥ Q J
	Pass	2 ♥	Pass	2 NT	♦ A 9 8 4 3
					♣ A J 8

You have 18 high-card points and a good five-card diamond suit. Even though partner's jump response indicates 11 or 12 points, easily enough for game, correct to 2NT. This leaves room for partner to express a preference.

3)	LHO	Partner	RHO	You	♠ A J 8
			1 ♦	Dbl	♥ K Q
	Pass	2 ♦	Pass	2 NT	♦ A 10 6 5
					♣ K Q 9 3

Partner's cue-bid is game-forcing. While slam is indicated, bid 2NT to complete the description of your hand.

When Is A Double For Takeout?

There are several conditions that must be met for a double to be for takeout rather than for penalty. First, your partner has not yet bid, but may have passed. Second, the takeout double can only be made at your first opportunity to double a particular suit; whenever you could have doubled earlier and did not, a later double of that suit is for penalty. Finally, at the game level, you need to be able to double for penalty; such doubles are primarily for penalty, not takeout.

1)	LHO	Partner	RHO	You
				Pass
	1 ♦	Pass	Pass	Dbl

You may double diamonds for takeout as this is the first opportunity to do so, and partner has not made a positive bid.

2)	LHO	Partner	RHO	You
	1 ♦	Pass	1 NT	Dbl

This is your first chance to double diamonds, consequently it is for takeout. Keep in mind though that the opposition appears to have at least half of the high-card values.

3)	LHO	Partner	RHO	You
	1 ♦	Pass	1 ♥	Dbl

Your double is for takeout, asking partner to bid the longer of the two unbid suits, where most of your strength lies.

4)   *LHO*   *Partner*   *RHO*   *You*
                                   1 ♦   Pass
         2 ♦   Pass   Pass   Dbl

> You could have doubled for takeout in the first round of bidding, but did not. Having passed up the first opportunity to double, this one a penalty double.

Takeouts are doubles of opponents' <u>*suit*</u> bids, not notrump. Hence doubling a notrump opening bid in not for takeout; it is always for penalty.

Takeouts After Preemptive Bids

All too often an opponent opens preemptively. A key tool to get your side into the bidding is the takeout double. These are classic takeouts because bidding space is not sufficient to pursue other types of takeouts. To compete effectively against preemptive openers, you must be willing to take risks, for it is sometimes impossible to judge whether you will be better off competing for the contract or ceding it.

         RHO   *You*   ♠ K J 10
         3 ♥   ??   ♥ 8 3
                                   ♦ A 9 8 2
                                   ♣ A 9 8 5

> You have 12 high-card points, and good distribution for a takeout. Of course if you double 3♥, partner must respond 3♠ or four of a minor, possibly without a single quick trick. There are approximately 20 high-card points unaccounted for, but who has them? You are put to a guess (which is why the opposition preempted). This hand is South in **Deal Number 30** (see page 173). South boldly doubles and is fortunate to find partner with a very good spade suit.

When an opponent preempts and you have minimum to good hand, you have no idea who has the missing honors. Quick tricks are golden and long suits comforting. Otherwise when an opponent opens preemptively, your side almost certainly has an eight-card fit, and your partner will have on average half of the outstanding honors.

The ideal distributions for classic takeout doubles are 4-4-4-1 and 5-4-4-0 with the shortness in the opponent's suit. This holds true no matter what the level, but at elevated levels, prudence suggests you have two additional points for each level above two that partner is likely to respond.

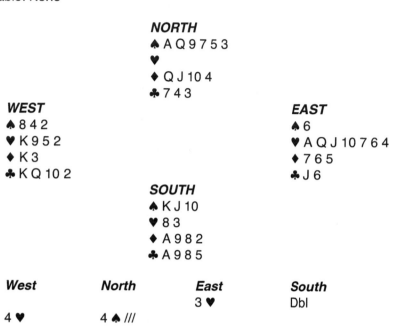

DEAL NUMBER 30

Dealer: East
Vulnerable: None

NORTH
♠ A Q 9 7 5 3
♥
♦ Q J 10 4
♣ 7 4 3

WEST
♠ 8 4 2
♥ K 9 5 2
♦ K 3
♣ K Q 10 2

EAST
♠ 6
♥ A Q J 10 7 6 4
♦ 7 6 5
♣ J 6

SOUTH
♠ K J 10
♥ 8 3
♦ A 9 8 2
♣ A 9 8 5

West	North	East	South
		3 ♥	Dbl
4 ♥	4 ♠ ///		

East opens preemptively. South has minimum opening values but an attractive distribution for a takeout double. West and North have not yet bid so it is not possible to gauge which side has most of the honors. Relying on his favorable distribution, South doubles and without hesitation North contracts for 4♠.

The play is straight forward. South loses only two clubs and one diamond, making his game. East-West can make 4♥ but they are overcome by the superior spade suit. South's double at the three level was a gamble, well rewarded by finding partner with a super hand.

After Weak Two Openers

Any hand that qualifies for a classic takeout at the one-level also qualifies at the two level.

1)   *RHO*   *You*   ♠ K J 9 7
        2 ♥   Dbl   ♥ 9 4
                                      ♦ A 7 6 4
                                      ♣ A Q 6

You have 14 points and good distribution for a takeout. This is about the minimum as partner will have to name a suit at the three-level.

2)   *RHO*   *You*   ♠ Q 9 8 5
        2 ♦   Dbl   ♥ A 10 5 4
                                      ♦ J 6
                                      ♣ A J 8

Life is replete with compromises. This hand is worth only 12 points, discounting the ♦J, but still worth the double as you can well accommodate any suit partner names.

Following Three and Four Level Preempts

Traditional preemptive openers require 6 to 10 high-card points, concentrated in the long suit - a seven-card suit to open at the three level, an eight-card suit to open at the four level. Some very aggressive players stretch these requirements, preempting with 5 points and shading the suit length by one. They are good candidates for penalty doubles. Nearly always when an opponent has a suit of seven or eight cards, your side will have a 4-4 or 4-5 fit, and often a 4-4 fit in two suits.

1)   *RHO*   *You*   ♠ A J 6 5
        3 ♦   Dbl   ♥ Q J 6 3 2
                                      ♦ 10
                                      ♣ A J 4

Hoping partner will answer you at the three-level, double with this 15 point hand. There is risk here, but more often than not you will have no regret.

2)   *RHO*   *You*   ♠ K Q 9 8
        4 ♣   Dbl   ♥ A K 7 2
                                      ♦ A 7 6
                                      ♣ 9 7

This 17-point hand is strong enough for game, particularly in a major where the odds of finding and eight-card fit approach 100%. If partner has his fair share of the honors, you have a good game try.

3)   RHO   *You*   ♠ K 7
     3 ♥   Pass   ♥ K J
                                 ♦ A 10 4 2
                                 ♣ A K 7 5 3

You have a strong, unbalanced hand, but after West opens 3♥, any bid you might choose is unsatisfactory. Spades are too short for takeout; clubs are too weak to overcall; diamonds may produce a good fit but there is no way to find out safely; notrump is tempting, but with only one heart stopper you could easily lose six heart tricks and a few others. This hand is North in **Deal Number 31** (see page 176).

IMMEDIATE CUE-BIDS

The methods of defensive bidding presented to this point enable you to compete with a wide range of hands up to about 20 points. What do you do with stronger hands, generally those that qualify for a strong two club opener, when an opponent opens first? The immediate cue-bid, that is bidding the opponent's suit, is the answer. It is artificial; you make no promise whatsoever regarding this particular suit. In fact you are likely to be short in the suit named, but not necessarily. The cue-bid announces great strength and is *forcing to game*, so you should have a good idea where the bidding should end. Please note that cue-bids do not apply to opponents' artificial (conventional) calls.

1)   *RHO*   *You*   ♠ A K 8 6
     1 ♦   2 ♦   ♥ K Q J 10 5
                                 ♦
                                 ♣ A K 4 3

This hand looks much like the classic takeout double, except that it is extremely strong. You have the potential to play in game and perhaps slam. You need partner's help in choosing trump.

2)   *RHO*   *You*   ♠ A K Q J 7 5
     1 ♥   2 ♥   ♥ 7 5
                                 ♦ A K
                                 ♣ K J 10

You are nearly certain of making a 4♠ contract. This immediate cue-bid distinguishes this hand as game-forcing and 21+ points.

DEAL NUMBER 31

Dealer: West
Vulnerable: None

NORTH
♠ K 7
♥ K J
♦ A 10 4 2
♣ A K 7 5 3

WEST
♠ Q 4
♥ A Q 9 8 7 6 4
♦ 7
♣ 10 9 2

EAST
♠ A J 10 9 6
♥ 5 3
♦ K 6 3
♣ Q 6 4

SOUTH
♠ 8 5 3 2
♥ 10 2
♦ Q J 9 8 5
♣ J 8

West	North	East	South
3 ♥	Pass	Pass	Pass ///

North has a very strong hand of 18 high-card points and honors in every suit. After West opens a preemptive 3♥, North has no satisfactory call. A takeout double is tempting but the spades are too weak. The clubs are too weak for an overcall at the four-level, besides diamonds could be a superior suit. Notrump could possibly produce a game contract, but there is only one heart stopper and no solid suit to run.

Against good defense, West loses two clubs and a ruff, a diamond and a Heart for down one. This is the best result North-South could achieve. They could not make 4♣ or 4♦, and in notrump they would lose at least six hearts and a diamond, going down three or more.

Responses

You must respond to partner's cue-bid no matter how poor your hand. Select a bid that shows your distribution.

1)

LHO	Partner	RHO	You	
1 ♦	2 ♦	Pass	2 ♠	♠ 10 9 7 6 4
Pass	3 ♥	Pass	3 ♠	♥ 7 5
Pass	4 ♠			♦ J 9 2
				♣ 8 7 4

Spades are your only assets. After partner identifies his suit with the 3♥ call, you must bid once more. This is a close call between rebidding spades and raising hearts. Selecting 3♠ keeps a notrump game open.

2)

LHO	Partner	RHO	You	
1 ♥	2 ♥	Pass	3 ♣	♠ 10 7 5
Pass	3 ♠	Pass	4 ♠	♥ 5 4 3
				♦ 9 4 3
				♣ Q 10 6 5

While you unfold this flat two-pointer, partner registers a cue-bid. Respond 3♣. Partner's second bid identifies his preferred spade suit. Raise to game.

*   *   *   *

Defensive Bidding - Winning Ways

OVERCALLS: You may shade your high-card points but your suit should be five good cards.

WEAK JUMP OVERCALLS: You may jump overcall with the same kind of hand with which you would open preemptively.

TAKEOUT DOUBLES: Use the takeout double with these three types of hands:
- Type I: Double with 11 or more high-card points and values in every unbid suit, aiming to accept any suit partner names.
- Type II: Double with a very good suit and 17+ points, aiming to show your suit at the next round.
- Type III: Double with a balanced hand, 19 to 20 points and stoppers, aiming to bid notrump next.

Following partner's takeout double you must respond unless RHO intervenes:

- With 0 to 5 points:
  - ✓ Bid longest suit available at the one-level.
  - ✓ Do not respond with 1NT.
- With 6 to 9 points, make a positive response:
  - ✓ Longest unbid suit.
  - ✓ With a stopper in the opponent's suit, bid notrump.
- With 11 to 12 points:
  - ✓ Jump-bid (one level) longest unbid suit .
  - ✓ Pass for penalty only when you have a strong stack of opponent's suit.
- With 13+ points:
  - ✓ Cue-bid opponent's suit.
  - ✓ Pass for penalty only when you have a strong stack of opponent's suit.

IMMEDIATE CUE-BIDS: With near-game values (21+ points), cue-bid opponent's suit, forcing partner   to answer.

14
COPING WITH INTERFERENCE

The focus here is how to proceed when your side opens and the opponents interfere in your otherwise orderly bidding process, for instance when partner opens and the next bidder (RHO) interjects a competitive call before you have an opportunity to respond. Now the tables are turned and the opposition is using the same tools you have used - takeout doubles, overcalls, and jump overcalls. Fortunately these actions create some new opportunities for your side, most notably redoubles and penalty doubles. There are hidden treasures to be mined here because so many rubber bridge players are loath to allow you to complete games and rubbers; and so they too frequently try to take away contracts that belong to your side.

Hypothetically, suppose a vulnerable opponent overcalls 2♦ and you double under circumstances where the odds are 70% in your favor because you have most of the honors and favorable distribution. If the opponents make the contract, they earn 80 points below the line and 50 above. Alternately, if you set the contract two tricks, you earn 500 points - thus winning 500 points 70% of the time and losing 130 points 30% of the time, hypothetically speaking of course. This is a reasonable enterprise unless your side misses a slam; but in that case you would have set them more than two tricks.

Contrast this result to a similar one where the opponents are not vulnerable. Setting them two tricks earns your side only 200 points, still losing 130 points when they make the contract. This 70 points is a marginal gain considering that you have given up a part-score or game in the process. Small margins can be the difference between a bottom and a top board in duplicate bridge, but they are not very attractive at the rubber bridge table.

This hypothetical example of alternative outcomes illustrates a key theme for coping with interference: that is to aggressively double for penalty when the opposition is vulnerable; and favor your own contract when they are not.

Often there are opportunities to profitably double game contracts as well as partials, particularly when the opposition reaches game or beyond through a hotly contested auction or by way of preemption, chiefly to prevent your side from obtaining a viable contract. More often than not you should double when you are at game and the opponents bid one more time. The time to be conservative, doubling only when you are near certain of a set, is when the double puts the opponents into a game they otherwise would not bid and could not make. You can be liberal with the double any time it does not put the opposition into game - contracts below 2♥ and contracts at game or higher.

AFTER A TAKEOUT DOUBLE

Right-hand opponent doubles (for takeout). You have the usual choices - bid a new suit, raise partner, or notrump - but the double opens a new powerful tool - the redouble. While this situation does not radically impact how you usually compete, there are some changes in emphasis that are of considerable moment. Since partner has another chance to speak, you do not need to go out of the way to keep the bidding open; thus you may pass with 5, 6 or 7 points if they do not appear useful given partner's opening suit. With intermediate values and little support for partner's suit, notrump is a most effective squelch of the opponents' aspirations. The redouble is reserved for strong hands where you want partner to know the hand belongs to your side one way or another, where you intend to either proceed to game or double the opponents for penalty.

Raises

It is tempting to think that the obvious thing to do is also the right thing, but not when it comes to the redouble. Here is the table scene: partner opens 1♥ and RHO calls "double" (for takeout). A redouble would put your side into a game contract requiring only seven tricks. Now suppose you have good heart support and 8 high-card points. This is a hand you would raise to 2♥ absent the intervening double. But what is the sense of raising to an eight-trick, part-score contract when you could be in a seven-trick game?

The problem with this scenario is that you are never, never allowed to play in a low-level, redoubled, game contract. The opponents always bid again if your partner doesn't. Here you have modest values in a competitive situation; the opponents have perhaps half or more of the high cards. If you do not describe this hand for partner immediately, he will be at a disadvantage trying to compete without knowing of your support and playing values. Thus contrary to doing the obvious, you should ignore the double and raise partner's major as you would sans the double; raise with 6 to 9 points, jump-raise with 11 or 12 points. Any other action allows opponents the chance to exchange information at a low level, quite possibly finding as good or better contract than yours, and especially when they have the spade suit.

It is a little more complicated when you have game values and support for partner's major. Now you need to distinguish hands rich in honors from those whose values are substantially distributional.

1)

Partner	RHO	You
1 ♥	Dbl	4 ♥

♠ 7
♥ Q J 8 7
♦ K J 7 3
♣ Q J 6 2

This is a nice hand in support of partner's hearts, one that warrants a game contract although it has just 10 high-card points. This triple jump makes it very difficult for the opponents to gauge what to do - double, overcall 4♠, or pass. Note that it is weak in defensive tricks.

2)

Partner	RHO	You
1 ♥	Dbl	Rdbl

♠ A 5
♥ Q 9 7
♦ 10 9 8 7
♣ A Q J 3

Here your hand has 13 high-card points, including strong defensive values in spades and clubs. You intend to either play this deal in a heart game or double for penalty whenever the opposition tries to run away with the contract.

New Suits

With hands of intermediate strength and a good suit, proceed as though there has been no interference. Any response at the one-level is forcing, and all subsequent bidding is the same as though there had been no double. In other words, ignore the double.

1)   *Partner*   *RHO*   *You*   ♠ 6 2
       1 ♣   Dbl   1 ♥   ♥ A K 9 7 3
                                               ♦ 9 5
                                               ♣ K 9 8 2

You have 10 high-card points and excellent hearts. Respond as though RHO had passed. If you do not bid hearts immediately, you may not be able to later.

2)   *Partner*   *RHO*   *You*   ♠ A Q 8 7 6
       1 ♣   Dbl   1 ♠   ♥ K 6 5
                                             ♦ 10 9 7 6
                                               ♣ 5

This hand is close to opening strength so the hand should belong to your side. Again you may respond naturally.

Notrump

Holding a modest or intermediate balanced hand (6 to 12 points), bid notrump after an intervening double. Given that notrump is both intimidating and consumes key bidding space, a good rule of thumb is to bid 1NT any time you are not sure what to do.

1)   *Partner*   *RHO*   *You*   ♠ K 8 6 5
       1 ♣   Dbl   1 NT   ♥ K J 7
                                             ♦ Q 7 5 2
                                             ♣ 6 3

It is a good sign when an opponent becomes annoyed at your bid, and that is what usually happens when you ignore the takeout double and bid notrump.

2)   *Partner*   *RHO*   *You*   ♠ 6 2
       1 ♥   Dbl   1 NT   ♥ Q 4
                                             ♦ Q 10 8 6 5
                                             ♣ A 9 7 3

You are not strong enough to bid 2♦ so the choice is between passing and 1NT. To pass is to concede the hand to the opponents.

3)   *Partner*   *RHO*   *You*   ♠ Q 10 8
       1 ♥   Dbl   2 NT   ♥ J 10
                                             ♦ K Q 6 2
                                           ♣ K 10 7 4

To make this call following a takeout double, you should have stoppers in all three unbid suits, and of course be short in partner's major.

Redoubles by the Responder

Any time you have 13 points and partner opens, your side has a clear margin of strength, sufficient for game or to prevent the opposition from taking the contract without being penalized. When this occurs and RHO doubles for takeout, you need to get this message to partner immediately so that he is positioned to participate effectively as the bidding progresses. The means to do this is the redouble, advising partner that you have game strength and that your side should not settle for less than a penalty double or a game contract. You may have support for partner's suit, but this is not necessary. The primary requirement is that you have great playing strength for either offense or defense.

	LHO	Partner	RHO	You	
1)		1 ♠	Dbl	Rdbl	♠ 6
					♥ Q J 6 2
	Pass	Pass	2 ♦	Dbl	♦ Q 9 5 3
					♣ A K 10 4

With both sides vulnerable, partner opens and RHO doubles. You have 12 high-card points and a spade singleton. This deal belongs to your side. A penalty double is promising as you will have four good trump in any suit the opposition selects. Should they pass out, your redouble gives you a near certain game and rubber. Having nothing but dregs, LHO passes the decision back to his partner. Unwilling to concede game and rubber, RHO runs to 2♦. Almost surely his diamonds are four and equally certain LHO has at most four diamonds. Now you double for penalty with confidence. Your hand is South in **Deal Number 32** where your side reaps 800 points from the penalty double (see page 184).

	LHO	Partner	RHO	You	
2)		1 ♥	Dbl	Rdbl	♠ A J 5
					♥ 7 4
	Pass	Pass	2 ♣	Dbl	♦ A Q 10 8 7
					♣ K Q 10

Even though vulnerable, RHO doubles for takeout. Surely with 16 high-card points you have an easy notrump game. Alternatively you have excellent prospects of a gigantic score from a penalty double. RHO has little more than two aces, a king and a 4-4 club fit. As these honors are in front of you, he may be unable to take more than four tricks.

	LHO	Partner	RHO	You	
3)		1 ♠	Dbl	Rdbl	♠ Q 8 5
					♥ K 6
	2 ♥	Pass	Pass	4 ♠	♦ A 2
					♣ K Q 9 6 2

DEAL NUMBER 32

Dealer: North
Vulnerable: Both

NORTH
♠ A K Q 9 5 2
♥ K 5 3
♦ A 10
♣ 8 2

WEST
♠ J 10 7 4 3
♥ 10 9
♦ 8 4 2
♣ J 7 3

EAST
♠ 8
♥ A J 8 4
♦ K J 6 3
♣ Q 9 6 5

SOUTH
♠ 6
♥ Q 7 6 2
♦ Q 9 7 5
♣ A K 10 4

West	North	East	South
	1 ♠	Dbl	Rdbl
Pass	Pass	2 ♦	Dbl ///

North opens a very good spade suit. Holding a minimum with an ideal
distribution for takeout, East doubles. With good defense against any
suit East/West may choose, and spade shortness, South redoubles.
Unable to save his partner, West passes and East runs to diamonds.
South doubles, expecting to gain a substantial penalty bonus.

Against the 2♦ contract, South leads to partner's spades; then over-ruffs
East on the spade return. South next leads three clubs, the ♣A, ♣K and ♣4,
North ruffing the third club. North leads his ♦A then ♠A, again ruffed by
East and over-ruffed by South. Finally East is able to win the ♣Q, the ♦K,
the ♥A, a heart ruff in dummy, and the ♠J - a total of five tricks, down three
doubled and vulnerable for -800.

Of course it is tempting to double 2♥ for penalty, but making game is nearly certain and you do not want to miss a possible slam.

Opener's Second Bid

Most often after partner redoubles you should pass to see how partner chooses to handle the opponent's takeout suit. This allows him the chance to make a penalty double if he so desires, or to show the direction further bidding should take. The time you should bid rather than pass is to show a hand with extra trump length and poor defensive values.

♠ 9 8	*You*	*LHO*	*Partner*	*RHO*
♥ 5 4	1 ♦	Dbl	Rdbl	1 ♠
♦ A K Q 10 4 2	3 ♦			
♣ K 9 4				

You have a great diamond suit, but on defense your hand will take only one diamond trick (maybe) and perhaps one club trick (50/50). This is not the time to look for a low level penalty double.

*   *   *   *

The redouble by responder has three important benefits. First, the redouble does not consume bidding space, allowing you maximum room to find the best contract. Second, by forcing LHO to bid, the redouble gives your side added knowledge that can aid in the play of the hand. Third, with game strength in your hands, it doesn't matter if the opposition holds the spade suit; if they choose to compete to the game level, a penalty double will reap oodles of points for your side.

Redouble by the Opener

As the opener, you may use the redouble to show strength well beyond a minimum opener. It must be noted however, that there are very few occasions where this tool is useful.

1)	*LHO*	*Partner*	*RHO*	*You*	♠ A 4
				1 ♦	♥ K 8 4
	Pass	1 ♠	Dbl	Rdbl	♦ A K Q 7 6
					♣ Q 7 6

Your redouble shows great strength, and presumably little or no spade support. The most likely outcome appears to be 3NT, but partner may be satisfied with this seven-trick game contract. Either you have an easy game or a substantial penalty score when the opponents run for cover.

2)	LHO	Partner	RHO	You	♠ A K 4
				1 ♣	♥ A 8 3
	Pass	Pass	Dbl	??	♦ 9 4
					♣ A K J 10 7

You have a powerful hand of 19 high-card points. However partner has
passed so you can expect no more than one-trick from his hand. You
have nowhere to go and a redouble will do nothing more than warn the
opponents to be careful. The better option is to pass and find out where
the opponents are headed.

AFTER AN OVERCALL

The adversarial overcall presents an environment different than the
takeout double. Now RHO is expected to have opening values and a
creditable five-card suit. When the honors are about evenly divided, the
party having the higher-ranked suit has the upper hand.

Responses With Supporting Hands

The first impulse when RHO interferes should be to raise partner's
suit when you have abundant support. Observe the same requirements
that apply to non-competitive direct raises.

After hearing partner open and RHO overcall, it is not often that
you see a hand with good support and more than 14 points. If you are
fortunate enough to pick up such a comely hand, you want to force the
bidding to game, and explore slam if you are so lucky. With 15 or 16
points, cue-bid the opponents suit to set up a game-force.

Partner	RHO	You	♠ J 7
1 ♥	1 ♠	2 ♠	♥ 10 8 6 5
			♦ A Q J 7
			♣ K Q 4

Your hand is worth 15 points in support of hearts. The cue-bid promises
game values and is forcing. Next you should raise hearts to game.

The jump shift (17 to 18 points) may be used after interference to
show a strong forcing hand. This is the same method you would use
without interference.

Partner	RHO	You	♠ K Q 9 2
1 ♠	1 ♥	2 ♠	♥ 6 4 3
			♦ A J 10 6
			♣ A K

You have 17 high-card points and quite satisfactory diamond support. The jump shift suitably describes this strength. Next you should raise to complete the description of your hand.

The other choice is the cue-bid, also game forcing. This bid requires 17+ points. It's special distinction is that it promises first or second round control of the over-caller's suit, an important distributional attribute for slam evaluation.

Partner	RHO	You	♠ K 6
1 ♥	1 ♠	2 ♠	♥ K 10 2
			♦ A 5 3
			♣ A K J 6 3

Your hand holds slam hope in hearts. First cue-bid RHO's spade suit. This alerts partner of your game intentions and slam interest. Typically you have a spade void or singleton, but K-x is a suitable substitute.

Responses With Non-Supporting Hands

You are contemplating what to do after partner opens and RHO overcalls when you do not have support for partner's suit. With RHO showing good values and a good suit, you should be a bit cautious until it becomes clear where most of the honors lie.

	Partner	RHO	You	♠ J 9 8
1)	1 ♣	1 ♦	1 ♥	♥ A K J 9 8
				♦ 8 7
				♣ 7 5 4

You have robust hearts and 9 high-card points. It is imperative that you show these hearts.

	Partner	RHO	You	♠ K J 7 5
2)	1 ♣	1 ♦	1 ♠	♥ A 3
				♦ 10 7
				♣ 10 9 5 3 2

Your primary interest here is to find out if there is a 4-4 spade fit. This hand is worth one exploratory bid so you had better call it immediately.

3)   Partner   RHO   You   ♠ 9 8 7
        1 ♣   1 ♦   Pass   ♥ K 4 3
                                                          ♦ 9 8 6 2
                                                          ♣ K 9 5

You have neither a biddable suit nor sufficient honors to make a free call.

4)   Partner   RHO   You   ♠ Q 7 6
        1 ♥   1 ♠   2 NT   ♥ 9 8
                                                          ♦ A J 10 7 6
                                                          ♣ K 10 8

With 10 high-card points, good diamonds, and a spade stopper, 2NT is
sure to silence the opposition.

Penalty Doubles After Overcalls

Overcalls are hazardous mainly because the overcaller may find a
partner with an anemic holding. It is rudimentary that when partner opens
and you have some 11 high-card points behind an overcaller, your side is
in firm control. RHO can salvage his hand only when he holds a long and
near-solid trump suit. Consequently a primary criteria for a penalty double
is that you have a good holding in RHO's suit that prevents him from
running trump. The other important criteria is that you lack support for
partner's suit, thus game your way is unlikely.

1)   Partner   RHO   You   ♠ Q 10 5 3
        1 ♥   1 ♠   Dbl   ♥ 8
                                                          ♦ A Q
                                                          ♣ Q 10 9 8 4 3

Partner opens 1♥, your short suit. When RHO overcalls spades, you are
looking at a hand that is worth perhaps only one trick on offense but three
or four on defense. This is a classic low-level double. Your hand is
South in **Deal Number 33** . East-West has no place to run and is set two
tricks doubled and vulnerable for -500 points (see page 189).

2)   Partner   RHO   You   ♠ 9 8 4 3
        1 NT   2 ♦   Dbl   ♥ 7 5
                                                          ♦ K Q J 3
                                                          ♣ J 7 4

Partner advertises 16 to 18 points and you have 7 points with strong
diamonds behind RHO. This is a time to weigh game prospects your
direction against a penalty double. Being a little short of a notrump
game, opt for the double.

DEAL NUMBER 33

Dealer: North
Vulnerable: East/West

NORTH
♠ K J 4
♥ A Q 6 5 3
♦ K J 9 7
♣ J

WEST
♠ A
♥ 10 9 4 2
♦ 8 5 4 2
♣ 7 6 5 2

EAST
♠ 9 8 7 6 2
♥ K J 7
♦ 10 6 3
♣ A K

SOUTH
♠ Q 10 5 3
♥ 8
♦ A Q
♣ Q 10 9 8 4 3

West	North	East	South
	1 ♥	1 ♠	Dbl ///

With five spades and 11 high-card points, East overcalls spades. Having no support for partner's hearts, South is tempted to bid his long club suit, but finally decides there is no game in sight for his side. On defense, he is likely to win 2 spades and 2 diamonds, and partner 1 or 2 hearts. If partner is short in clubs, there is a good chance of cross-ruffing hearts and clubs. Opponents are vulnerable so a set of one or two tricks will pay off handsomely.

On lead, South plays his singleton heart to partner's ♥A. On the heart return, South ruffs declarer's ♥K. Now South tries to get to partner via clubs, but declarer wins. Declarer's plight looks bleak. He plays trump to the ace and returns a club, but his ♣A is ruffed by North. North wins the ♥Q, playing another heart for South to ruff. When the dust settles, declarer is able to win 1 club trick and 4 trump, for down 2 doubled and vulnerable, and -500 points.

Misfits

When your side has a misfit, odds are high that the other side has one too. Listen to the bidding carefully; often the opposition has trouble finding a good strain, confirming your suspicion of a misfit.

1)	♠ 4	*You*	*LHO*	*Partner*	*RHO*
	♥ K 7 6 5	1 ♣	Pass	1 ♠	Pass
	♦ A 2	2 ♣	Pass	Pass	2 ♥
	♣ A K Q 8 2	Dbl			

Thinking your side is showing weakness by stopping at 2♣, RHO imprudently and belatedly enters the fray with a 2♥ overcall. Your partnership does not have a good fit and it appears the opposition does not either. Holding the balance of quick tricks your way, the penalty double looks like a money-maker.

2)	*LHO*	*Partner*	*RHO*	*You*	♠ 4 3 2
		1 ♦	Pass	1 ♥	♥ K Q 6 5
	Pass	1 NT	Pass	Pass	♦ 3 2
	2 ♣	Pass	Pass	Dbl	♣ A 8 6 4

With 60 points below the line and no fit, you are content to play 1NT for game. LHO cannot allow game that cheap so he pushes with a balancing 2♣ overcall. Double and make him pay a hefty fine if he cannot make the contract.

3)	*LHO*	*Partner*	*RHO*	*You*	♠ 7 6
		1 ♦	1 ♥	Pass	♥ K Q 9 6
	1 ♠	Pass	2 ♥	Pass	♦ 4 3 2
	2 ♠	Pass	3 ♥	Dbl	♣ A K 3 2

RHO insists on his long hearts, while LHO appears short or void in them. Your partner obviously has spades behind LHO (because you and RHO are short in spades). Thus the opponents have misfits in the majors and your side has most of the honors and both minors - an excellent time to double even though it puts them into a game contract.

Contested Game Auctions

Competition to game provides good opportunities for penalty doubles. Any time your side has genuine game values and the opponents preempt or bid once more to prevent you achieving game, do not let these bids stand unchallenged - if it is not safe to bid again, double.

1) ♠ K Q 10 7 5   *You*   *LHO*   *Partner*   *RHO*
    ♥ A 7 4   1 ♠   2 ♦   3 ♠   4 ♦
    ♦ 3 2   4 ♠   Pass   Pass   5 ♦
    ♣ A Q 10   Dbl

You have a strong opener. When partner jumps to 3♠, there is a sound game contract. LHO pushes to 5♦, apparently to thwart your game. With these defensive tricks, pass only if RHO is your spouse!

2) *Partner*   *RHO*   *You*   ♠ Q J 4
    1 ♦   4 ♠   Dbl   ♥ A 3
                                            ♦ J 7 4 3
                                            ♣ 5 4 3 2

Possibly your side can make 5♦. But this is precarious and you have two sure tricks on defense. Double even though there is an outside chance that 4♠ can make.

3) ♠ A K 7 6 5   *You*   *LHO*   *Partner*   *RHO*
    ♥ 6 2   1 ♠   2 ♥   2 ♠   4 ♥
    ♦ J 9 8   ??
    ♣ K Q 3

Should you bid 4♠ or double? You have 13 high-card points, very good for offense, also good for defense. If partner has some 8 to 10 high-card points, a penalty double would be appropriate. The key point here is you do not know whether partner has a minimum or a maximum, so either a 4♠ bid or a double is speculative. Since you have a minimum and have already shown it, you should pass the final decision to partner,

AFTER A JUMP OVERCALL

Perhaps there will always be bridge players who prefer strong jump overcalls in preference to weak, preemptive jump overcalls. When you encounter them, your hand will not have many honor values (between your partner with an opener and RHO with a strong hand, there are at most 9 high-card points for you and LHO to share). The usual choice following a strong jump overcall is to pass unless you are able to merely raise partner' suit.

The focus here is on opponents who employ weak jump overcalls. These overcalls are harmful to your orderly bidding - as of course they are meant to be. Now a simple raise may take you to the three-level and a jump raise to the four-level, in either case one step higher than you would have freely elected to bid.

Partner	RHO	You	♠ 7 5 3
1 ♥	2 ♠	??	♥ Q 7 5
			♦ A J 8 6 2
			♣ 5 4

This is a hand with which you would not hesitate to raise partner's 1♥ to 2♥. However RHO inserts a jump overcall making it impossible to shape a normal raise.

Following a weak jump overcall, you may raise partner's suit with several points less than you would in a non-competitive auction. With the hand shown above, raise to 3♥ with this eight-point hand. Seemingly this advice contradicts the notion that you need 11 or 12 points in support of partner to contract for nine tricks. However analysis of random deals proves this practice to be statistically valid. The specifics of this analysis are presented in **NOTE 3: Raising After An Opponent's Jump Overcall**, page 205. The guidelines from this analysis are:

- With support and 6 to 9 points, raise to the three-level
- With support and 11 or 12 points, jump raise to the four-level.

If you raise to the three-level with 6 to 9 points and play for nine tricks, you should succeed 70% to 85% of the time. If you raise to the four-level with 11 or 12 points, you should succeed 70% to 80% of the time. These are very good, competitive odds.

These guidelines reflect the fact that partner nearly always has more than a minimum opener. This is inevitable because there are a lot of distributional points around the table and, by his weak jump overcall, RHO is known to have very few honor points. Someone has to have the cards and on average you will find that partner has 16 points; and this validates the guidelines.

1)	Partner	RHO	You	♠ Q 6
	1 ♥	2 ♠	3 ♥	♥ 10 7 3
				♦ K J 10 5
				♣ J 9 4 2

You have 7 points and support for partner's hearts. This hand has the values to raise to 3♥. This is the South hand in **Deal Number 34** where North continued to a 4♥ game (see page 193).

DEAL NUMBER 34

Dealer: West
Vulnerable: None

NORTH
♠ A 7 4
♥ A Q 6 5 2
♦ 9 3 2
♣ A K

WEST
♠ 5 2
♥ K J 8
♦ Q 7 6 4
♣ Q 10 8 3

EAST
♠ K J 10 9 8 3
♥ 9 4
♦ A 8
♣ 7 6 5

SOUTH
♠ Q 6
♥ 10 7 3
♦ K J 10 5
♣ J 9 4 2

West	North	East	South
Pass	1 ♥	2 ♠	3 ♥
Pass	4 ♥ ///		

North opens a heart and East overcalls 2♠ (weak jump overcall). South has
three-card support for hearts and 7 high-card points. This is the range
for a single raise, so South calls 3♥. North has 17 high-card points. This
may be enough for game if partner has a good 9-point raise. Having no
way to test the waters, North takes a chance on game.

Reluctant to lead from his K-J of spades, East leads a small club, declarer
taking the trick with his ♣A. Hoping to find East napping with the ♠K, declarer
plays a small spade toward the ♠Q in dummy. If East does not come up
with the ♠K immediately, declarer will make the contract with two spades
and a ruff (West over-ruffs but then North takes all five hearts), 2 clubs and
the ♦K. Unfortunately (for declarer) East takes the first spade with the ♠K.
Now declarer loses 2 diamonds (ace and queen), 1 heart and ♠K. Down one.

2) | Partner | RHO | You | ♠ 10 9 5 2 |
      | 1 ♠ | 3 ♦ | 4 ♠ | ♥ K Q 8 |
      | | | | ♦ 6 5 |
      | | | | ♣ A 6 3 2 |

You have 12 points, sufficient to raise to game after RHO shows a weak, preemptive hand.

3) | Partner | RHO | You | ♠ 10 7 4 |
      | 1 ♥ | 3 ♠ | ?? | ♥ Q 8 7 |
      | | | | ♦ A J 6 5 |
      | | | | ♣ 7 4 2 |

This 7-point hand is worth a raise to 3♥, but this bid is no longer obtainable following RHO's preemptive jump to 3♠. If you are not vulnerable, 4♥ may be a good sacrifice. However, when vulnerable, a pass is in order since the odds of making game are not favorable.

Notrump

The standards for notrump bids after an overcall are substantially the same as without the interference, except of course you need a stopper in the overcaller's suit. At the one-level, the standard 1NT response is 8 to 10 points. A jump to 2NT represents 11 or 12 points, and a jump to 3NT represents 13 to 15 points.

Partner	RHO	You	♠ K J 5
1 ♣	2 ♥	3 NT	♥ K J 9 6
			♦ Q 5
			♣ A 10 4 2

With adequate heart stoppers and 14 high-card points, notrump game is an appropriate undertaking. On the other hand, if the opponents are vulnerable, a penalty double could hook a whale-size bonus.

*   *   *   *

Coping with Interference - Winning Ways

When the opponents are vulnerable, aggressively double for penalties; but when they are not, favor your own contract.
- Holding a poor to moderate hand, consume as much bidding space as you can, raising or calling notrump.
- With a good suit and moderate strength, bid your suit.
- Redouble when you have 13 points and great playing strength.

A
ETHICS AND ERRORS

Suppose your partner opens and RHO overcalls. If you are quick to pass when your hand is a bust but slow to pass when your hand has a little merit, this innocent action can but should not aid partner in deciding how far to compete for the contract. We all strive to make our calls apace so as to not divulge information not contained in the call itself; however bridge is a complicated game and most of us amateurs. Sometimes it is hard to figure out what to bid; other times we have two or three choices and cannot make up our mind. The pace of our action, or inaction, sometimes gives clues, clues that go beyond the stated bids, thus divulging what is referred to as "unauthorized information".

Proper table ethics require you to tune out partner's smiles and frowns, or other mannerisms that may allow you to infer something about his or her hand. Of course you cannot entirely avoid observing partner's mannerisms, but you can and should ignore them and make the calls you would have otherwise. The rubber bridge game is intended foremost as an enjoyable, social past-time. To protect this objective requires only that the participants base their actions solely on authorized information.

At one time or another most of us inadvertently err at the table, perhaps by bidding out of turn or making an illegal call. When an error occurs, the common remedy is to back up and correct the mistake, then continue bidding. Those who play strictly according to "Hoyle" and those who play for substantial sums should comply strictly with the **Laws of Contract Bridge**, published by the American Contract Bridge League.

Here are some guidelines, consistent with the "Laws", for social bridge play that provide remedies for the most common bidding problems.

Insufficient Bid

West opens 1♥ and an inattentive North says 1♦! Being insufficient, North must correct the bid to one ranking higher than 1♥. The usual and proper correction is for North to revise his bid to 2♦ and that is the end of the matter. If North insists that 2♦ would not be appropriate and chooses some other call, South gains information about his partner's hand, and consequently must pass throughout the auction.

195

Pass Out-Of-Turn

Occasionally at the beginning of an auction someone forgets who is the dealer and passes before it is his turn. This is a minor infraction and easily remedied by restarting the bidding correctly at the dealer's seat. The person who erred then repeats his pass at his turn to bid.

Bid One Seat Out-Of-Turn

Suppose East is the dealer when South, second to bid, mistakenly opens 1♣. The bidding reverts back to East. South should then repeat his bid (1♣ is this instance) when his turn arrives. If South is unable to repeat the same call because East's action has made it insufficient, South should make his call legal by bidding clubs at whatever level is required to make it legal. If South selects any other action, his partner must pass throughout the remainder of the auction.

Bid Out-Of-Turn Before Partner's Turn

Suppose West or North is the dealer when South opens 1♣ out of turn. This error is one of the more difficult to resolve fairly because his partner, who must bid before South, has been made aware of South's opening strength and distributional character. The official rule requires North to pass throughout the auction, a harsh penalty. An informal alternative, if acceptable to the players at hand, is to restart the bidding and trust North to ignore his partner's error and bid as though the error had not occurred. (This is not nearly so difficult as it may seem.)

Unintended Call

Sometimes you are thinking ahead or whatever, and inadvertently make a call you did not intend. You may change it to the one you had in mind and bidding continues without penalty. However this correction must be made as soon as you realize that you meant to say something else, and certainly before the next player makes a call.

Special Bidding Treatments

It is fundamental to the game of bridge that you have access to the meanings of your opponents' bids, just as they have between themselves. It is quite improper to have private understandings about certain bids or bidding sequences. Generally **Standard American 21** employs natural bids that do not require explanations. Moreover, if your bridge group adopts **Standard American 21** as the common system, you avoid potential problems of private understandings and special bidding treatments, one of the objectives of this book.

Bridge protocol requires partnerships to state in advance their general approach to bidding, or to explain their system if it is something other than standard. During play, you have a right to inquire regarding the meaning of any particular bid. When an explanation is to be made, it is always the partner of the person making a call who is asked to provide the explanation; it would be quite improper for the person making a call to also explain it because he may also be enlightening his partner in the process.

.

B
SCORING

The first side to score 100 points below the line wins a game. When a game is won, both sides begin the next game with no score below the line. The first side to win two games wins the rubber and the rubber premium. At the end of the session, the side holding the only game or the only part-score is credited with unfinished rubber premiums.

TRICK VALUES (Below the line)
For each trick bid and made beyond six:

	Not *doubled*	*Doubled*	*Redoubled*
Majors - each trick	30	60	120
Minors - each trick	20	40	80
Notrump			
1st trick	40	80	160
Each additional trick	30	60	120

OVERTRICKS (Above the line)
For each trick made beyond the contract:

	Not *doubled*	*Doubled*	*Redoubled*
Not vulnerable			
Minors	20	100	200
Majors & Notrump	30	100	200
Vulnerable			
Minors	20	200	400
Majors & Notrump	30	200	400

HONORS (Above the line)
Honors include A, K, Q, J, 10. Honors can be earned by either side:

Four trump honors in one hand	100
Five trump honors in one hand	150
All four aces in one hand in a notrump contract	150

SLAMS (Above the line)

	Not Vulnerable	Vulnerable
Small slam bid and made (12 tricks)	500	750
Grand slam bid and made (13 tricks)	1000	1500

UNDERTRICKS (Above the line)
For each trick declarer falls short of a contract:

	Not Vulnerable		
	Not *doubled*	Doubled	Redoubled
First under-trick	50	100	200
Second & third under-trick	50	200	400
Each additional trick	50	300	600

	Vulnerable		
	Not *doubled*	Doubled	Redoubled
First under-trick	100	200	400
Each additional under-trick	100	300	600

PREMIUM SCORES (Above the line)

Winning a rubber (opponents not vulnerable)	700
Winning a rubber (opponents vulnerable)	500
Having the only game in an unfinished rubber	300
Having the only part-score in an unfinished game	100
Making a doubled contract	50
Making a redoubled contract	100

C

NOTES

NOTE 1: FIVE-CARD MAJORS VS. NOTRUMP

The question is, when your hand qualifies to open either a major or 1NT, which is the better choice? These are hands that contain a five-card major, are balanced (5-3-3-2 distribution), and are valued at 16 to 18 points. Ever since the introduction of five-card majors, bridge authorities have differed in their recommendations as when to open the major and when to open notrump. Notably, William Root and Max Hardy both advised that the choice depended on the particular distribution of honors in the opener's hand, however they disagreed as to the specific criteria. Also they cautioned against opening notrump when the two-card suit was without honor (the infamous worthless doubleton). In stark contrast, Marty Bergen, in "Points Schmoints" advised to always open 1NT, irrespective of the internal character of the hand, so long as it satisfies the notrump requirements. While possible, it seems unlikely that these conflicting recommendations would produce equal or nearly equal results. Bridge in the 21st century needs more clarity than this.

When partner opens his five-card major and you have three or more, you know immediately where to play the contract; it remains only to decide how high to go. Usually this scenario produces straightforward bidding sequences. However when you do not have support, the strong opener may have difficulty describing his strength when he has more than a minimum and not quite enough for a jump shift - these are hands of 16 to 18 points.

The rebid problem is most acute when you open 1♥ and partner responds 1♠. After this sequence your next bid either understates or overstates your strength; a second bid of 1NT shows only a minimum opener while a jump to 2NT or a jump shift shows 19 or 20 points. Alternatively, when you open 1NT, partner is immediately aware of your strength but has no indication of the existence of a five-card major. Hence when a hand qualifies to open a major and notrump, the best choice apparently depends upon the character of the responding hand, which of course is unknown.

The first step in resolving this conflict is to segment the deals into three subsets, each having to do with the amount of support responder has for your major. These subsets are:

- Responder has inadequate support (less than three)
- Responder has better than three-card support
- Responder has exactly three-card support

Responder Has Inadequate Support

If you held a strong opening hand and knew in advance that partner had fewer than three of your five-card major, you would not hesitate to open 1NT, for without a fit, there is nothing to gain by opening the major. Being more accurate in describing strength, 1NT makes subsequent bidding easier; and in the event opener's suit is hearts and responder has spades, a good spade fit easily can be found using the Jacoby Transfer Convention.

Responder has less than three-card support in 41 out of 100 random deals. This subset favors opening 1NT because there is no wasted bidding on an unsupported major suit.

Responder Has Better Than Three-card Support

When responder has four or more support, you should prefer to play in the nine- or ten-card major rather than notrump. If you knew in advance of these excellent fits, of course you would open the major. On the other hand, these fits are readily found after a notrump opener by using the Stayman Convention, in which case the notrump opener will promptly identify his five-card major (promising at least four). In this manner, every 5-4 and 5-5 combination is easily found. Thus by applying Stayman, the pair can always find the same major suit contract that would have been found by opening the major.

These good fits occur 30 out of 100 times. Since they can be found equally well after both major and notrump openings, they are neutral regarding the choice of opener.

Responder Has Exactly Three-card Support

The third possibility is to find responder with exactly three-card support, producing 5-3 major suits. When the major is opened, invariably the contract is played in the major; when notrump is opened, most often the contract is played in notrump.

In competitive bidding, notrump has considerable preemptive value. When the opponents compete for the contract, the notrump opening has a deterrent value toward silencing the opponents.

♠ K 9 5 4 2   If RHO opens 1 heart, you have a good takeout double.
♥ 5   Alternatively if RHO opens 1NT, you would be reluctant
♦ A 9 6   to overcall at the two level with this poor spade suit.
♣ A Q 4 3

The notrump opener has an advantage because opening 1NT puts you into contracts that produce better scores 63 times per 100 deals, most of them by small margins of 10, 20, or 40 points. However small, these are margins that are crucial in match-point scoring.

Of special significance in rubber bridge, notrump openers produce good game contracts about 10% more often than do major openers. The predominant reason for this outcome is that suit contracts require one more trick for game, yet balanced hands (5-3-3-2) do not always produce that extra trick.

These 5-3 fits occur 29 of 100 deals, and they favor opening 1NT by a small but persistent margin.

The Worthless Doubleton

It is perfectly acceptable to open 1NT with a two-card suit that has no honor card, a suit that is often referred to as a worthless doubleton. For some this has been a determinant for preferring a major instead of 1NT. Sometimes it pays off - if you open the major whenever you have a worthless doubleton, you get a better score 36% of the time. The bad news is that you get a poorer score 64% of the time. Why? There are three circumstances that favor notrump contracts.

- Two-thirds of the time partner has the needed control in your weak suit.
- The opponents cannot find your weak suit soon enough.
- When the opponents do find your weak suit, often distribution is such that they can take only four tricks in that suit.

Conclusions

Two of the subsets containing deals that occur 70% of the time favor opening notrump. The other subset where responder has better than three-card support is neutral because either choice leads to the same contract. Furthermore, where there is a 5-3 fit and the strong hand contains a worthless doubleton, notrump still produces better results by a margin of two to one.

Although the rules of **Standard American 21** allow you the option of opening a major suit or 1NT whenever the hand meets the requirements of both, _notrump is the recommended option_.

Some bridge players have preferences regarding suit contracts verses notrump contracts. If you prefer playing suit contracts, you may certainly modify the recommendation without serious detriment to your partnership. If you do, the suggested compromises are:

- Open a major when your suit is spades because the rebid decision is less difficult than it is when the suit is hearts.
- Open a major when your honors are concentrated in one or two suits.

NOTE 2: MAJOR SUITS - JUMP RAISES TO GAME

While hand evaluation rules were less precise in the olden days, it was well recognized that the fourth and fifth trump in responder's hand opposite opener's five-card major were of considerable, but unspecified, extra value. Hence a common practice was to jump raise directly to game with hands that were light in honors and long in trump. This practice was viewed as somewhat preemptive yet with expectations of making the contract. It is now known that game prospects may be accurately predicted by including trump-length distribution points in hand evaluation. *Standard American 21* employs the double jump when responder's points total 13 or 14, without distinction between distribution and honor characteristics because the odds of making are equally good.

This modern practice of fast arrival raises a new concern. If the opener is strong enough to consider slam (19 points or so), need he be concerned as to whether partner's values are equally valid at the slam level irrespective of the distribution or honor content, provided of course the partnership has at least three aces?

Two responder hands were selected for this test. One was this hand from *Goren's New Contract Bridge Complete*:

♠ x
♥ K J x x x
♦ Q J 10 x x
♣ x x

In support of hearts, this hand has 7 high-card points and 7 distribution points. Opposite a 1♥ opening, Goren advises a jump directly to 4♥.

The other hand is from Chapter 6 - The Majors (page 73):

♠ J 10 6 5 2
♥ K 9 4 3
♦ A 9 4
♣ 6

In support of spades, this hand has 8 high-card points and 6 distribution points. A double jump to 4♠ is recommended following a 1♠ opening.

Both of these hands were matched with randomly generated hands of 18 to 21 high-card points and a five-card major, hearts in the first instance and spades in the second instance. After excluding matched pairs with less than three aces, the remaining pairs were analyzed to determine how many tricks they likely would produce. If a trick depended upon a finesse working, it was credited as ½ trick.

Both of these tests produced the same results - 12 or 13 tricks could be taken 63% of the time. Perhaps some bridge players would settle for games rather than risk slams and be set one-third of the time, but this success frequency is well within a range that most competitive players find acceptable. At any rate, the purpose of the analysis was to determine if distribution points, especially those derived from extra trump length, are valid at the slam level, and the findings confirm that they are. Also confirmed as sound practice is the use of the limited (13 to 14 points) double-jump raise.

NOTE 3: RAISING AFTER AN OPPONENT'S JUMP OVERCALL

When you have support for partner's opening suit and RHO interferes with a weak jump overcall, you may raise partner's suit with less points than is needed to raise in a non-competitive auction. Statistical analysis supports this practice. When RHO makes a weak jump overcall and you have support for partner's suit and 6 to 12 points, the odds of taking nine or ten tricks are:

Responder's Strength	Nine Tricks	Ten Tricks
6 or 7 points	70 to 75%	20 to 25%
8 or 9 points	80 to 85%	40 to 50%
11 or 12 points	95 to 100%	70 to 80%

As you see here, holding 6 to 9 points opposite partner's opening hand, you can expect to take nine tricks 70% of the time or more, certainly sufficient to raise to the level of three. Furthermore, with invitational strength (11 or 12 points) you should be able to take ten tricks at a frequency of 70% or higher.

While these statistics seem to be at odds with the normal bidding rules when there is no interference, they reflect the fact that nearly always partner has more than a minimum opener. How so, you may ask? The weak jump overcall is preemptive and is typically made with a six-card or longer suit. Invariably when one hand is distributional in nature, others are also, and the total hand values exceed 40 points by some significant margin.   These points are somewhere.   With the hand to your right claimed weak and your hand limited, you should expect partner to have several points more than a minimum - about 16 points on average. Consequently you are fairly safe in "borrowing" two or three points from partner's hand and raising accordingly.

Any time your chances of success in bridge are better than 60% (or 70% if you are conservative), go for it. The recommended guidelines after a weak or preemptive jump overcall by RHO are:

- With support and 6 to 9 points, raise to the three-level
- With support and 11 or 12 points, jump raise to the four-level.

These guidelines produce bids one level higher than non-competitive raises.

LaVergne, TN USA
09 February 2011
215915LV00003B/69/A